BERNIE'S BROOKLYN

BERNIE'S BROOKLYN

HOW GROWING UP IN THE NEW DEAL CITY SHAPED BERNIE SANDERS' POLITICS

THEODORE HAMM

OR Books
New York · London

All rights information: rights@orbooks.com
Visit our website at www.orbooks.com
First printing 2020

Published by OR Books, New York and London

Excerpted lyrics from "Mermaid's Avenue" Words by Woody Guthrie, Music by Frank London. © Woody Guthrie Publications, Inc. & Nuju Music. (BMI) Excerpted lyrics from "My New York City" Words and Music by Woody Guthrie. © Woody Guthrie Publications, Inc. Excerpted lyrics from "Hanukah Tree" Words by Woody Guthrie, Music by Frank London. © Woody Guthrie Publications, Inc. & Nuju Music. (BMI)

Library of Congress Cataloging-in-Publication Data: A catalog record for this book is available from the Library of Congress.

Map by Urwah Ahmad (2020).

paperback ISBN 978-1-68219-240-5 • ebook ISBN 978-1-68219-243-6

CONTENTS

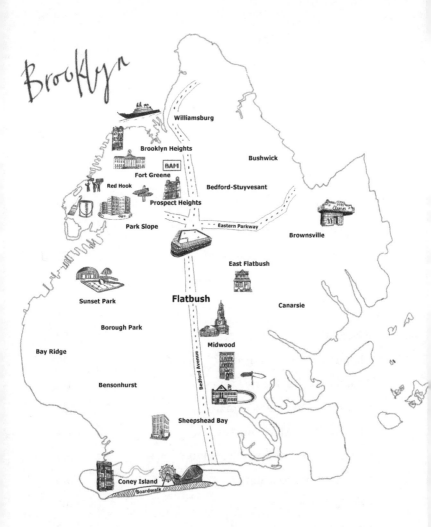

Brooklyn Navy Yard

 31 Grace Court
Arthur Miller Residence
(1947-1951)

 Brooklyn Borough Hall

BAM Brooklyn Academy of Music

 Striking Longshoremen

 Atlantic and Flatbush
Intersection

 St. Joseph's Cathedral
(Pacific and Vanderbilt)

 Red Hook Houses
(Grand Opening Ceremony
July 4, 1939)

 71 Otsego Street
HQ of Keystone Paints
(Eli Sanders' Employer)

 WPA Swimming Pool
(Opened 1936)

 Woody Guthrie Residence (1950-1952)
Beach Haven Apartment Complex
(Owned by Fred Trump)

 Woody Guthrie Apartment
(1943-1950)
3520 Mermaid Avenue

 Ebbets Feild

 5224 Tilden Avenue
Jackie Robinson
(1947-1949)

 Brooklyn College

 Bernie's Home
1525 E. 26th Street

 Intersection of Kings Highway
and Nostrand Avenue

 James Madison High School

 Parkway Theater on Pitkin Avenue

INTRODUCTION

After Bernie Sanders won the popular vote in the Iowa caucus, the first primary in the 2020 presidential election, panic among Democratic Party elites and their allied corporate media commentators reached a fever pitch. "Bernie Sanders isn't a Democrat," exclaimed Bill Clinton adviser James Carville, adding that Sanders has "never been a Democrat. He's an ideologue." Carville specifically called Bernie's plan for free college tuition "a stupid thing."[1] One of Carville's colleagues from the 1992 Clinton campaign then opened the New Hampshire televised primary debate with a similar focus. ABC's George Stephanopoulos prodded Joe Biden into explaining why he had asserted Sanders is "too big a risk for the Democrats," to which Barack Obama's vice president replied, "Bernie has labeled himself . . . a democratic socialist." Shortly thereafter, Stephanopoulos— whose salary is $15–$17 million per year—asked for a show

1   Sean Iling, "'We're Losing Our Damn Minds': James Carville Unloads on the Democratic Party," *Vox* (2-7-2020).

of hands among the six candidates if they "were concerned about having a democratic socialist at the top of the ticket." ("I'm not!" Bernie declared.) While only the centrist candidate Amy Klobuchar echoed Biden's concern, had oligarch Michael Bloomberg been on the stage, he surely would have joined in. After the debate, MSNBC's Chris Matthews, a former top aide to longtime Democratic Speaker of the House Tip O'Neill, jumped the shark, comparing Bernie to Fidel Castro and raising the specter of "executions in Central Park" if Sanders takes the White House. And during that same week, 2016 Democratic candidate Hillary Clinton continued her vengeful crusade against Bernie, warning that it was not "responsible" for any candidate to "promise the moon."[2]

The contempt for Bernie's democratic socialist vision is further illustration of how far the Democratic Party has moved from FDR and the New Deal. Like many key figures in his administration, Roosevelt was a Keynesian capitalist, not a socialist. Neither were the coterie of middle-class reformers FDR brought to Washington from New York City's settlement house movement of the Progressive Era. But the New Deal's policies were not simply the handiwork of far-sighted technocrats. Instead, FDR's team responded to pressure exerted from below. The Great Depression

2   Matt Willstein, "Hillary Clinton Redoubles Bernie Sanders Attack on 'Ellen': Need Someone 'Who Can Win,'" *The Daily Beast* (2-6-2020).

had spawned both labor militance, leading to a strike wave that shut down the West Coast waterfront in 1934; and social movements, including the retirement pension campaign led by Dr. Francis Townsend that had launched a year earlier. In 1935, both efforts helped create two of the New Deal's most enduring legacies: the right for unions to organize and strike (as stipulated by the Wagner Act) and the Social Security system. Yet when FDR and prominent allies such as New York City mayor Fiorello La Guardia spoke of the president's "social security program," the lowercase term referred to far more than simply pensions. As FDR outlined in his "Economic Bill of Rights" (1944) and other speeches, he viewed it as the federal government's responsibility to provide jobs, health care, and secure housing for the American people. Rather than democratic socialism, FDR created a blueprint for social democracy akin to what exists in many European countries today.

Many fundamental elements of Bernie's 2020 agenda—including free college tuition, rent control and massive federal investment in housing, and vast public works projects that provide public-sector jobs (now the Green New Deal)—were realities in the Brooklyn where he grew up. Although FDR viewed health care as a right, and his successor Harry Truman began to push for national health insurance soon after he took office in 1945, no universal medical care system was implemented. But New York City had a vast, low-cost network of health care

accessible to both union members and non-union households such as the Sanders family. While Bernie's proposal
for Medicare for All is thus an extension of a landmark
initiative of the Great Society, LBJ's administration essentially continued to enact FDR's domestic blueprint. As historian Kim Phillips-Fein demonstrates in *Fear City* (2017),
the Wall Street-led response to New York's fiscal crisis of
the mid-1970s helped launch the neoliberal agenda of pri-
vatization within the Democratic Party. The same Clinton
crowd that championed neoliberal "Third Way" rollbacks
of New Deal policies not coincidentally loathes a candidate that adheres to FDR's principles. As Bernie, who was
born in 1941, stated in a November 2015 campaign speech
at Georgetown University about democratic socialism,
FDR stressed in his Second Bill of Rights speech that "real
freedom must include economic security" "That was
Roosevelt's vision seventy years ago," he declared. "It is my
vision today."[3] During that same campaign, Bernie's older
brother, Larry (b. 1935) explained that the siblings and
their peers grew up "in an environment where New Deal
politics were quite normal. It was widely understood that
the government could do good things."[4] With post-Reagan
Republicans deriding all social spending, and post-Clinton

---

3   For transcript, see *Vox* (11-19-2015).

4   Kevin Kelley, "Bernie's Bro: Bernie's Working-Class Brooklyn Roots Shaped
    My Brother," *Seven Days* (5-27-2015).

Democrats fetishizing private sector solutions to public problems, the origins of the Sanders brothers' view of government's positive potential is well worth exploring.

Socialism, of course, comes in many different varieties, and the one that most influenced the Sanders brothers in their early years was distinctly tied to their religious heritage. By 1950, nearly one million Jews lived in Brooklyn. The Sanders family was part of a Jewish enclave near Kings Highway in Midwood, which was then considered to be a section of the larger neighborhood of Flatbush (which had a large Irish Catholic population). While Larry and Bernie's father, Eli Sanders, had immigrated from modern-day Poland in 1921, their mother, Dorothy "Dora" Glassberg, was born in New York City and went to high school in the Bronx. Dora's father was a committed socialist and a union activist in the garment industry. As the historian Daniel Katz has argued, the perspective that grew out of that working-class milieu during the early twentieth century is best understood as Yiddish Socialism. Rather than a doctrinaire set of views regarding political strategy, adherents shared a strong set of cultural values, including that government should provide basic necessities, all ethnic and racial groups should be treated equally, and all people should be able to develop their full potential through education. Such aspirations became signature features of the New Deal's "social security program." As Katz explains,

in the wake of the anti-Communist hysteria of the early
Cold War period, the native-born generation of Jews coming of age in the 1950s like the Sanders brothers experienced the "transition from Yiddish Socialism to Jewish
Liberalism,"[5] which tempered expectations surrounding
the role of government in creating equality. Although neither Eleanor Roosevelt nor her close ally—and two-time
Democratic presidential candidate—Adlai Stevenson
were Jewish, both were revered figures in Bernie's neighborhood. The first political event Bernie recalls attending
was a Stevenson rally held at his elementary school when
he was in eighth grade.

During the New Deal through the end of World War
II, the two most important political figures in New York
City were FDR and his close ally, Mayor Fiorello La Guardia
(1934–1945). With FDR's administration providing a
steady stream of funding, La Guardia and the urban plan-
ner Robert Moses built modern New York City. Among the
"good things" La Guardia's administration constructed
during the period were the city's grand W.P.A.-funded outdoor swimming pools, as well as hundreds of playgrounds,
including one right around the corner from the Sanders
family's home. After New Deal money dried up amid
the war effort, La Guardia and Moses created a blueprint

5   Daniel Katz, "The Key to Bernie Sanders' Appeal Isn't Socialism. It's
Yiddish Socialism," *The Forward* (2-14-2016).

that the latter enacted after the war, which included vast expansion of the city's public housing system, what's now JFK Airport, and a dizzying array of expressways (many of which proved to be not at all good for the neighborhoods they sundered). Led by its dynamic labor movement, New York City in the two decades after World War II became what historian Joshua Freeman has called "a social democratic polity . . . committed to an expansive welfare state, racial equality, and popular access to culture and education." As just one of many examples, the City University of New York (CUNY) underwent a vast expansion in the 1950s and 1960s and did not charge tuition until the aftermath of the fiscal crisis of the mid-1970s. For working-class people and lower-middle-class families like Bernie's, CUNY provided the opportunity for social mobility. In the mid-1950s, Larry Sanders attended Brooklyn College, where he became politically active and influenced his younger brother to follow suit. While their mother was ill, Bernie attended the same CUNY school, where he was first introduced to the work of his favorite historical figure, Socialist leader Eugene Debs.

While New York remained a social democratic city through the 1950s, Brooklyn became a central presence in American culture. In American arts and letters, on the baseball diamond, and in living rooms across the country, Brooklyn was a familiar place. By the early 1950s,

Brooklyn-based novelist Norman Mailer, playwright Arthur Miller, and poet Marianne Moore were household names. Eli Sanders, a paint salesman, directly identified with the struggles faced by Willy Loman, Miller's signature character. In April 1947, Jackie Robinson broke the color line in America's national pastime at Ebbets Field, a place frequented by Larry and Bernie. From the middle of the war through the early 1950s, Woody Guthrie called Coney Island home. The songwriter memorably depicted a place full of summertime joys but also residential segregation, a practice enforced by his racist landlord Fred Trump. Woody's music would travel with Bernie through Vermont onto the 2016 campaign trail. By the time Bernie graduated from high school, most of the leading cultural figures of the past decade had moved out of Brooklyn. And so too had the Dodgers, a betrayal that scarred a generation. Like many of his peers, Bernie left Brooklyn during his college years and returned only periodically. But in ways far deeper than simply his accent and mannerisms, Brooklyn never left Bernie.

One of the remarkable features of New York City in the middle three decades of the twentieth century was the plethora of political parties that wielded influence. There were the Democrats, still controlled by Tammany Hall in Manhattan along with similarly Irish-led machines in the Bronx and Brooklyn. The Republicans of the era had a vocal Progressive wing, of which La Guardia was the most prominent figure. Vito Marcantonio, who eventually took over La Guardia's East Harlem congressional seat, became a leading figure in the American Labor Party, which had been formed by FDR's allies in the garment unions in 1936 in order to minimize the influence of the Norman Thomas-led Socialist Party. The Communist Party worked closely with the ALP, which caused the split within the latter party in 1944 that gave rise to the Liberal Party. The mix produced very strange bedfellows, with the ALP joining Governor Tom Dewey's Republicans in supporting the campaign of Woody Guthrie's Communist pal Jimmy Longhi for a Congressional seat representing the Brooklyn waterfront. The ALP also helped Dewey, a pro-big business Republican, enact New York's statewide system of rent control in 1950. La Guardia's successor, Brooklyn Democrat William O'Dwyer, left amid scandal that same year. For the next four years, City Hall was controlled by a candidate who had won on the ballot line of the newly created Experience Party. The numerous parties and unexpected alliances placed the period in sharp contrast to the staid two-party politics that have dominated both New York City and the nation for the last several decades.

What follows is a journey into the complex politics and lively culture of the Brooklyn that produced Bernie Sanders. It is meant to be a popular history, aimed at conveying key moments as they were experienced by Bernie, Larry, and their peers. There are both major events affecting everyone in the city and smaller details documenting Bernie's youth. What happened behind the scenes in the city and borough's corridors of power is not a primary concern. For example, most of Robert Moses's backroom dealings during the period only came to light upon publication of Robert Caro's landmark work *The Power Broker* in 1975. Throughout the 1950s Moses certainly made many enemies in the Bronx and Greenwich Village, but his direct impact on Bernie's neighborhood was minimal. While they certainly help shed light on the important events of the era, neither the *New York Times* nor the *Brooklyn Daily Eagle* were read in the Sanders family's home. Instead, the paper of choice was the then-liberal *New York Post*, which during Bernie's high school years featured an all-star lineup of political columnists (Max Lerner, Murray Kempton, and Eleanor Roosevelt) and sportswriters (led by Milton Gross and Jimmy Cannon). Under publisher Dorothy Schiff and editor James Wechsler, the paper's Cold War liberalism helped shape the sensibility of Bernie's generation. In addition to the recollections provided by Larry and those published elsewhere from Bernie, the following chapters include insights from a number of friends of Bernie and a variety of peers. Brooklyn was a quite remarkable place in the mid-twentieth century. Onward into its past we go.

PART ONE

CHAPTER ONE: FDR AND LGA

Although FDR had easily defeated Wendell Willkie in the 1940 presidential election, the contest in both candidates' home state of New York was surprisingly close. Willkie, backed by the liberal Republican Eastern Establishment, came within just three percentage points of winning. FDR's wide margins in Brooklyn, Manhattan, and the Bronx carried him to victory (Willkie won Queens and Staten Island). The president captured nearly 750,000 votes in Brooklyn, roughly 350,000 more than his challenger—and FDR only won the state by 225,000. In the Midwood state assembly district where the Sanders family lived, the Democratic ticket took home nearly 75 percent of the vote. As Larry Sanders recalls, his parents enthusiastically voted for FDR and the family's immediate surrounding area was "99 percent pro-Roosevelt."

The pending entry of the United States into World War II had been a recurring issue throughout the fall campaign, and FDR thus made the transition to a wartime economy the initial subject of the first State of the Union address of his third term. But that same speech in early January of 1941 is most remembered for the "Four Freedoms," the quartet of promises made on both the domestic and international front. What FDR stated in the passages preceding those vows is also most noteworthy. He declared:

Certainly this is no time for any of us to stop thinking about the social and economic problems which are the root cause of the social revolution[,] which is today a supreme factor in the world.

For there is nothing mysterious about the foundations of a healthy and strong democracy. The basic things expected by our people of their political and economic systems are simple. They are:

Equality of opportunity for youth and for others.

Jobs for those who can work.

Security for those who need it.

The ending of special privileges for the few.

The preservation of civil liberties for all.

FDR here boldly outlined a contract between the U.S. government and its people, one that followed eight years in which the New Deal had put millions of people to work, established the Social Security system, and created numerous worker protections (including the right to join a union). The following winter, in the wake of Pearl Harbor, FDR and his administration would initiate the large-scale deprivation of civil liberties for Japanese Americans. But his January 1941 vow further clarifies the contradiction between the racist exclusion of Japanese internment and Roosevelt's democratic ideals.

Before defining the four freedoms, FDR further delineated his vision of what the U.S. government should provide to its people. He declared that "Many subjects connected with our social economy call for immediate improvement," and as examples stated:

We should bring more citizens under the coverage of pensions and old-age insurance.

We should widen the opportunities for adequate medical care.

We should devise a system by which a person deserving or needing gainful employment may obtain it.

Such efforts would require revenue, of course. In the spirit of "personal sacrifice," FDR said, Americans should be prepared for the "payment of more money in taxes." Input from individuals was thus necessary to provide for the greater collective well-being of American society.

Buoyed by the flow of revenue, Congress could then advance FDR's four freedoms, both at home and abroad. As the president explained:

The first is freedom of speech and expression—everywhere in the world.

The second is the freedom of every person to worship God in his own way—everywhere in the world.

The third is freedom from want—which, translated in world terms, means economic understandings which will secure to every nation a healthy peacetime life for its inhabitants—everywhere in the world.

The fourth is freedom from fear—which, translated in world terms, means a world-wide reduction in armaments to such a point and in such a thorough fashion that no nation will be in a position to commit an act of aggression against any neighbor—anywhere in the world.

No chief executive in the United States can unilaterally establish Constitutional rights, of course. So what FDR outlined here is best referred to as a set of governing principles. Even as the Nazis' imperial terror threatened Europe's democratic future, FDR outlined a postwar blueprint similar to that eventually followed by the United Nations, the growth of which both he and First Lady Eleanor Roosevelt championed. Though by no means always practiced, the principles espoused by FDR promised a democratic, egalitarian future.

FDR had moved into the White House in 1933 after consecutive two-year terms as governor of New York. The patrician figure with a grand family estate on the Hudson enjoyed close ties to the Progressive Era reformers who had come of age trying to improve conditions in the slums of New York City's Lower East Side. Many of the pivotal figures who shaped New Deal policies thus came from the nation's largest city. Frances Perkins, FDR's secretary of labor (as well as the first female cabinet member in U.S. history), had first gained public influence in the aftermath of the calamitous 1911 Triangle Shirtwaist Fire. Harry Hopkins had been a social worker on the Lower East Side before taking over the city's Bureau of Child Welfare in 1915. During the New Deal, Hopkins ran the Works Progress Administration (WPA), which indelibly altered the social and physical landscape of the entire country, not least in New York City.

The pivotal figure steering the New Deal in the city was Fiorello La Guardia. Standing all of 5'2" tall, the charismatic figure variously known as the "Little Flower" (after the Italian translation of Fiorello) or "Major" (his army air service rank during World War I) was a one-man melting pot. That his mother was Jewish and his father was Italian enabled him to appeal to the largest new immigrant groups that had been inhabiting the city since the late nineteenth century. That he was a practicing Episcopalian helped endear him to the city's WASP elite. In New York's 1933 mayoral election, that same elite helped La Guardia, a progressive Republican, triumph over the Irish-controlled Tammany Hall machine. New York City's most colorful and successful mayor of the modern era thus represented a political coalition quite unique to its time—and most unlike any formations in the city or state today.

Born in 1882 to immigrant parents in Greenwich Village, La Guardia experienced first-hand the perils of corruption when his father, a U.S. Army bandmaster, was poisoned by contaminated meat during the Spanish-American War of 1898. Shady government suppliers passed along "embalmed beef," preserved with spices and chemicals, to the military. La Guardia never forgave the "crooked army contractors" he viewed as responsible for his father's premature death. After completing his undergraduate work at New York University, he attended NYU Law, joined the bar and set up a private practice. Unsuccessful in his first bid for Congress in 1914 in Greenwich Village, La Guardia defeated the Tammany candidate two years later. His career was interrupted by WWI, but he returned to Congress after winning the 1922 race in East Harlem, then a working-class Italian and Jewish neighborhood. A Socialist candidate, Morris Hillquit, had won majorities in the Jewish sections of the district in 1920. La Guardia combined a fair number of those votes with a strong showing among Italians.

But amidst the Roaring Twenties, La Guardia was an outlier in the laissez-faire Republican Party of Harding, Coolidge and Hoover. In the words of the radical historian Howard Zinn:[6]

---

6   Born in 1922, Zinn grew up in Brownsville and Williamsburg before attending Thomas Jefferson High School in East New York. During World War II, he worked at the Brooklyn Navy Yard.

He set his stocky build and rasping voice against all the dominant political currents of the day. While the [Ku Klux] Klan membership soared into the millions, and nativists wrote their prejudices into the statute books, La Guardia demanded the end of immigration restrictions . . . Above the jubilant messages of the ticker tapes, La Guardia tried to tell the nation about striking miners in Pennsylvania. As Democrats and Republicans lumbered like rehearsed wrestlers in the center of the political ring, La Guardia stalked the front rows and bellowed for real action.

Progressive Era stalwart Senator Robert La Follette of Wisconsin continued to lead the most pro-labor wing of Republicans, and while in Congress over the next five terms La Guardia worked closely with him. Ex-president Teddy Roosevelt was also a Progressive Republican figurehead during the same period, and he supported La Guardia's unsuccessful run for New York City mayor in 1929. But the Little Flower first and foremost placed himself in the tradition of the party's towering figure. "I stand for the Republicanism of Abraham Lincoln," La Guardia declared in his 1922 campaign, adding, "I am a Progressive."[7]

Like Manhattan and the Bronx, Brooklyn, the city's most populous borough (and the state's largest county),

7   Howard Zinn, "La Guardia in the Jazz Age," *The Politics of History* (Boston: Beacon Press, 1970), 103–104.

was overwhelmingly Democratic.[8] In his 1932 loss to FDR, Republican incumbent President Herbert Hoover captured only 25 percent support in Kings County.[9] But in his successful Republican mayoral bid one year later, La Guardia—running on an anti-Tammany, anti-corruption platform—tallied over 43 percent in Brooklyn. La Guardia won the race with a 40 percent citywide total, with two Democratic candidates splitting the vote. In casting their lot with La Guardia, the city's upper-class voters had united with the new immigrant blocs of its working class; the former opposed Tammany on the grounds of corruption and inefficiency, while the latter fought back against their exclusion by Tammany and its counterpart Irish-dominated machines that similarly controlled Democratic politics in the Bronx and Brooklyn. Though no friend of Tammany, FDR had refrained from crossing the aisle and openly supporting his friend La Guardia during the campaign. But once the Little Flower took office, that relationship fully bloomed.

La Guardia made it clear from the jump that he was ready to partner with FDR's administration to rebuild a

8   As journalist John Gunther noted, by the end of WWII Brooklyn "deliver[ed] the biggest Democratic vote in the nation." John Gunther, *Inside U.S.A.* (New York: Harper & Brothers, 1947), 554.

9   New York City-based Socialist candidate Norman Thomas ran for president in 1932. Brooklyn provided him with just over 50,000 of the 120,000 votes Thomas received in his hometown. He finished with 4 percent in New York State and 2 percent nationwide (tallying nearly 900,000 votes).

city ravaged by the Great Depression. In *City of Ambition* (2013), historian Mason B. Williams writes:

> *Only days after his election, La Guardia assembled groups of architects, engineers, and other experts to develop proposals for everything from a city airport to park improvements, from subway extensions to public art projects, public housing to municipal beer gardens, promising [Harry] Hopkins that they would be put into operation on the first day of his administration.*[10]

The incoming mayor further clarified that Robert Moses would be the point man in his administration, overseeing the proposed massive investments in public works. Moses had gained widespread popularity during the 1920s as head of the Long Island Parks Commission under FDR's predecessor, Governor Al Smith. Moses built the interconnected parkway (or highway) system leading from the city to the grand Jones Beach recreation area he designed on the southern shore of Long Island. Moses, a devotee of "expertise" in government and thus no friend of Tammany, had endorsed La Guardia in the 1933 campaign. An odd couple of sorts—one a surly technocrat, the other a charismatic showman—Moses and La Guardia quickly began transforming the New York City landscape.

---

10 Mason B. Williams, *City of Ambition: FDR, La Guardia, and the Making of Modern New York* (New York: Norton, 2013), 154.

With substantial funding from Hopkins and the Civil Works Administration, La Guardia and Moses first targeted the city's dilapidated parks. By the end of April 1934, an army of workers had overhauled the Central Park Zoo and painted every park bench in the city. By mid-September, a former Board of Transportation storage yard in Midtown had become Bryant Park. Those projects helped create public support for the creation of the WPA in 1935. Under Hopkins's direction, the WPA put several million people to work across the nation building projects including the Tennessee Valley Authority and Camp David. Over six thousand writers created in-depth tour guides to states, cities, and regions, more than five thousand artists created grand public murals, and no less than fifteen thousand actors and countless musicians provided a vast range of mostly free performances. From the National Negro Theatre in Harlem to summer concerts in Brooklyn's Prospect Park, the WPA became an active presence in the cultural life of the city.

La Guardia and Moses also invested WPA money in major public works. In the summer of 1936, the Parks Department opened a total of eleven new Olympic-sized outdoor swimming pools across the city. On a balmy evening in mid-July, an excited crowd of fifty thousand Brooklynites came to see Mayor La Guardia (along with Moses) at the opening ceremony for the Sunset Park pool.

At that time the neighborhood of Sunset Park was primarily Scandinavian but also had Irish, Italian, and Polish enclaves, and the location of the pool was close to adjacent Borough Park, which was increasingly Jewish. "So enthusiastic was the gathering," the *Brooklyn Eagle* reported, that the police had to restrain people "from breaking into the pool grounds and mobbing the speakers' rostrum." Each dignitary was given a two-minute time slot, making it one of the shortest speeches of the Little Flower's career. "This is the finest swimming pool in the country," he told the cheering crowd, "and it's all yours." He then flipped the switch that turned on the $1.25-million pool's underwater lights. A diving troupe from the Parks Department rounded out the festivities with a series of what the *Eagle* called "fancy and comic dives."[11]

As the enormous crowd at Sunset Park illustrated, La Guardia and Moses were delivering the goods to city residents. Moses, in turn, used the popularity of such projects to further maximize his control over the city's landscape. During the 1930s, as Robert Caro explained in *The Power Broker*, Moses possessed "immense popularity" as well as "immense influence" in Albany. Moreover, the Little Flower benefited from "Moses's ability to ram through the

11 *Brooklyn Daily Eagle** (7-21-1936). The pool was originally open from 10 a.m.–10:30 p.m. Kids under fourteen got in free until 1, then had to pay ten cents. Adult admission was twenty cents. All eleven WPA pools are still open in the summer and are free for everyone. *Hereafter, *Brooklyn Eagle*.

great public works the Mayor, as sculptor of the metrop-
olis, desperately wanted rammed through."[12] Legendarily
arrogant, and certainly not a proponent of racial equality,
Moses dismissed critics who asked why more playgrounds
weren't being built in Harlem and other black neighborhoods. This conflict put La Guardia in a bind, because he
needed black votes and strived to maintain his anti-racist
reputation. Both the mayor and the builder thus turned
out for the opening ceremony for what was then called the
Colonial Park Pool (now Jackie Robinson Pool) in Central
Harlem in August 1936. An enthusiastic crowd of twenty-five thousand area residents attended an event that
featured Bill "Bojangles" Robinson performing his signature tap dance moves. The mayor urged "the knockers"
(i.e., critics) of his administration's efforts in Harlem "to
come around and look at this pool," which also featured a
dazzling underwater lighting system.[13] Several new playgrounds would be built in black neighborhoods including
Harlem and Bed-Stuy over the next five years, suggesting that the knockers' pressure on La Guardia and Moses
brought results.

Providing large new public amenities certainly had
political benefits for La Guardia, who coasted to reelection

---

12   Robert A. Caro, *The Power Broker: Robert Moses and the Fall of New York*
     (New York: Vintage, 1975), 636.

13   *New York Times* (8-9-1936).

against Tammany-backed Democrat Jeremiah Mahoney in 1937. The uninspiring challenger, a former judge, helped the mayor frame the race as pitting an accomplished reformer against a sputtering Democratic machine. Mahoney accused his Republican incumbent of "Communistic" policies, at one point claiming that La Guardia had belonged to the same organization as Vladimir Lenin.[14] The Little Flower, meanwhile, touted the parks, swimming pools, and new school buildings constructed in his first term; and he urged voters not to let Tammany get its mitts on New Deal money. La Guardia took home 60 percent of the November citywide tally, winning the Democratic stronghold of Brooklyn by over 200,000 votes—or 63 percent of the total. (One year earlier, FDR—for whom La Guardia campaigned—had scored 76 percent of the borough's vote in his landslide reelection.) "Democratic Leaders Fail to Ring the Bell" read the headline in the *Brooklyn Eagle,* which reported that the dynamic Republican mayor had won 21 of the 23 assembly districts in the borough.[15] In the predominantly Jewish South Brooklyn neighborhood

---

14 *Brooklyn Eagle* (10-29-1937). The basis of Mahoney's claim was that La Guardia and Lenin had both been stockholders in the Russian-American Industrial Corporation, an entity created by the New York City-based Amalgamated Clothing Workers union in 1922 to promote garment manufacturing in the Soviet Union. Lenin died in 1924 and the manufacturing initiative ended a year later, but La Guardia's endorsement for reelection by the Communist Party fueled Mahoney's red-baiting.

15 *Brooklyn Eagle* (11-3-1937).

where the Sanders family lived, the margin of victory for
La Guardia exceeded 2–1.[16]

La Guardia's reelection also illustrated the depth of
his support from the city's large union membership. The
American Labor Party had been formed in New York State
in 1936 to back FDR but not align with Tammany. (The
state's fusion voting system allows parties to cross-en-
dorse candidates from other parties, providing the same
candidate with multiple ballot lines.) Prior to the ALP's
formation, Sidney Hillman, national leader of the clothing workers—and a pivotal figure in the creation of the
C.I.O.—met with both La Guardia and Eleanor Roosevelt,
who signed on to the plan to create a new party designed
to peel off labor support for the Norman Thomas-led
Socialist Party. The leader of the ALP was David Dubinsky,
president of the International Ladies Garment Workers
Union. He described his 400,000 members (more than
half of whom lived in New York City) as "all Socialists," and
the ALP successfully delivered those votes first to FDR and
then to La Guardia.[17] Given that the needle trades work-
force was largely Jewish and Italian, the Little Flower was
clearly their candidate. Historians calculate that in the

16 The vote in Brooklyn's 2nd Assembly District, which included the Sanders
    family's neighborhood, was roughly 69,000–33,000 in favor of the La
    Guardia, the highest total and widest margin of any the borough's districts.
    Ibid.

17 For a discussion of ALP and La Guardia, see Williams, 219–220.

1937 election, La Guardia received 69 percent of the city-wide Jewish vote, 63 percent from Italians, and 70 percent from blacks.[18] Over 480,000 voters supported the mayor on the ALP line, effectively providing the Little Flower's margin of victory; in Brooklyn, La Guardia reeled in just over 200,000 of the party's votes, only 27,000 less than he received on the Republican line. The mayor's advocacy for unions and the entire working class during his first term clearly paid dividends at the ballot box.

Though not a union household, the Sanders family knew the influence of the labor movement well. Born in 1912, Dorothy (or Dora) Sanders was the daughter of Benjamin and Bessie Glassberg, both of whom had immigrated from Russia in the first few years of the twentieth century. Dora attended high school in the Bronx. As Larry Sanders explains, Benjamin was a cloak presser in the city's large garment industry—a skilled trade dominated by men because it involved very heavy machinery. Glassberg, a socialist, was active in Local 35 of the New York Cloak Pressers Union; his son Willie (b. 1902, aka Phillip) was

18 For vote totals, see Williams, 232. Though he was a congressman from East Harlem, La Guardia did not receive the support of the area's black leaders in his unsuccessful 1929 run for mayor. But prior to his victorious second bid, La Guardia forged close ties with influential black labor leader A. Philip Randolph; in the wake of the 1935 Harlem riot, the mayor developed a strong working relationship with Adam Clayton Powell Jr., who at that time was an influential minister in Harlem. See Wil Haygood, *The King of the Cats: The Life and Times of Adam Clayton Powell, Jr.* (New York: HarperCollins, 2006 ed.), 46–49.

also a cloak presser. According to historian Daniel Katz, writing during the 2016 presidential campaign, Bernie's version of socialism is best understood as the "Yiddish Socialism" that migrated from Czarist Russia and found its home in the garment industry unions that led the New York City labor movement from the period just before the Triangle Shirtwaist Fire of 1911 through World War II. The "dominant political and cultural current among the working-class Jews of Brooklyn" during the period, Yiddish Socialism called for multicultural solidarity via unions and political parties, and it placed a high value on the arts, culture, and education.[19] Larry Sanders agrees that these were values the family shared with their Brooklyn peers, recalling that his grandfather was known to hold forth at family gatherings about the benefits of socialism. Although Benjamin Glassberg died in 1940, one year before Bernie was born, it's hardly a stretch to say that Yiddish Socialism is in Bernie's DNA.

The FDR-La Guardia-Moses alliance continued apace during the president and mayor's respective second terms, with La Guardia famously serving as the intermediary between FDR and the master builder (who hated one another because Moses was closely connected to Al Smith, FDR's nemesis). La Guardia made a point of flying back and forth from the city to DC—where he'd tell the president a

19 See Katz.

sad story about the hardship of city residents, then return home with an additional $50 million in New Deal funding[20]—in order to build public support for the city's first airport, which was named for the mayor and opened in October 1939. The new airport was just one of many projects built during the Little Flower's second term. In August 1939, the New York office of the WPA issued a press release listing a dizzying array of accomplishments since the preceding summer. Renovations were taking place at 18 public schools and 27 hospitals, over 150 handball courts and 8 skating rinks had been constructed, and more than fifty miles of new sewers and more than thirty-three miles of new power lines were put in place.[21] Literally and figuratively, the WPA was laying a new foundation for New York City.

Since the spring of that same year, the city of the future had also been on display near La Guardia Airport. Over the preceding four years Moses had steered the creation and promotion of the 1939 World's Fair at Flushing Meadows. FDR and La Guardia each spoke at the opening ceremony, which was the first event broadcast on live television in New York. Millions of city residents and tourists flocked to

20 Ric Burns's *New York: A Documentary Film* (2001) presents the FDR anecdote well. See Episode 6: "City of Tomorrow (1929–1941)."

21 See WPA press release (8-16-1939). Available here: http://kermitproject. org/newdeal/wpa-nyc-1938.html.

see exhibits including GM's car-based city (which Moses helped design) and featuring technological marvels such as FM radio, fax machines, and a seven-foot-tall robot that smoked cigarettes. WPA laborers built the fairgrounds, and they were also responsible for the opening that year of Randall's Island Stadium, Orchard Beach in the Bronx, and Jacob Riis Beach in Queens. Given the dark clouds encircling Europe, 1939 was an oddly sunny moment in the city's history.

Published by Random House that same year, the *WPA Guide to New York City* conveyed the atmosphere of neighborhoods across the city, including the Flatbush/Midwood area where the Sanders family lived. The committee overseeing the Federal Writers Project featured several leading figures in New York City publishing, including Brooklyn native Clifton Fadiman; and among the authors of the local guide was the rising literary star Richard Wright, who at the time lived in Fort Greene and soon married a Communist organizer from Brooklyn named Ellen Poplar (*née* Poplowitz). Wright penned the *Guide*'s Harlem section, and well over half of the work's 625 pages cover Manhattan. The Brooklyn section provides a brief but telling description of the Sanders family's neck of the woods. "Flatbush is one of Brooklyn's most desirable residential neighborhoods," the entry began. "[M]ost of the tree-bowered streets," observed the *Guide*, "have a tranquil, late-19th century air." Many streets featured "roomy homes" with "spacious front porches," although there were "numerous modern apartment houses." The book presented Midwood as a section of Flatbush. There the Sanders family lived in one of the newer, more modest dwellings. Completed in 1932, 1525 E. 26th Street is a large six-story building with eighty-eight units, and the Sanders family rented a small three-and-a-half room apartment on the second floor (2C). In general, the Midwood area saw significant growth after the Brighton Beach subway line (now the B/Q train) began traveling directly to Manhattan in 1920. Although the *Guide* depicted the area as tranquil, the hostilities in Europe would soon disturb the peace in Flatbush. But the suburban values of the area nonetheless endured.[22]

July Fourth of that year brought the usual fireworks display at Coney Island, and it also saw the opening ceremony for the Red Hook Houses near Brooklyn's thriving docks. The project was built by the New York City Housing Authority (NYCHA), which had been created by La Guardia in 1934 and was the first public housing agency in the nation. The $13-million Red Hook project was the second complex built in Brooklyn (the first, in Williamsburg, had opened in 1938) and fourth in the city. A crowd of 1,500 people turned out on Independence Day to see the mayor

22 *The WPA Guide to New York City* (New York: Random House, 1939), 492–493.

speak. Public housing was "quite in line with our form of government," the Little Flower declared. Then, anticipating FDR's Second Bill of Rights speech, he stated:

I do not believe it was contemplated by the framers of our Constitution that certain individual rights—freedom of assembly, free speech, free press, and freedom of religion—should be guaranteed and that the people should be abandoned and that people should be permitted to suffer in an emergency [i.e., lack of affordable housing]. It is my belief that in addition to the maintenance of these rights it is the responsibility of government to provide economic security for all.

FDR, added La Guardia, shared that position, as illustrated by his request to Congress that year to increase funding for public housing. Construction of the Red Hook project had begun only one year earlier, and although only 114 families were moving in on July 4, the entire 2,500-unit complex would be completed by Thanksgiving.[23]

Like the other NYCHA projects of the era, the Red Hook Houses were nevertheless anything but hastily built, cheap construction. Instead, the blueprint illustrated the harmonious vision of modernist architectural design. Drawn up by noted architect Alfred Easton Poor, who would later serve as president of the National Academy of Design, the Red Hook buildings were six stories and contained

---

23 *Brooklyn Eagle* (7-5-1939).

spacious units with ample sunlight. The complex also featured courtyards with playgrounds, as well as nursery centers and community meeting spaces. A year after the project's completion, residents entering the project's main building encountered *A Blueprint for Living*, a large mural created by WPA-sponsored artist Marion Greenwood, a Brooklyn native who studied in Mexico with Diego Rivera and Jose Clemente Orozco. The work, which won praise from Eleanor Roosevelt during her visit to the Red Hook Houses in June 1940, depicted what Greenwood described as "a community plan." As described by the *Brooklyn Eagle*, the first panel of the 325-square-foot triptych "suggests the healthful environment of the planned community, with its facilities for rest, recreation, study, and cultural activities," with the latter two panels emphasizing the labor that constructed such a project and the families that would benefit from it.[24] Together, NYCHA and the WPA were trying to build a secure future for the city's working class.

Public housing was indeed a central focus of La Guardia's second term. Precisely as the Red Hook Houses were completed in November 1939, new plans were unveiled for NYCHA complexes in Fort Greene, near the

24 *Brooklyn Eagle* (7-17-1940, 10-11-1940, 11-8-1940, and 11-28-40).
    At the formal unveiling of the mural in late November, Marion said the time
    she spent creating the mural was "a swell experience."

Brooklyn Navy Yard. The mayor announced that the new development would be the "largest and most daring housing project ever accomplished by this or any other city in this country." What distinguished the new initiative was its height, with buildings ranging between six and thirteen stories high; but it also featured comprehensive neighborhood planning. As the *Brooklyn Eagle* explained, there would be over 3,000 units "with plenty of sunlight and air, with playgrounds, schools, and health centers . . . [which] will give the whole of Brooklyn a new sense of dignity."[25] Although NYCHA construction would largely subside during the war (then increase exponentially during the postwar period), the Fort Greene complex was one of the few projects completed during La Guardia's third term. It was opened in February 1944 as two distinct NYCHA entities, the Whitman and Ingersoll Houses. Though the two provided a combined total of more than 3,400 units, or 300 more than the Queensbridge Houses (opened in 1940), the Queens location holds the distinction as the largest single housing project in both the city and nation. Unlike Ingersoll and Whitman, Queensbridge followed the lower-rise blueprint of Red Hook. Critics would soon

25 *Brooklyn Eagle* (11-22-1939). In her seminal work *The Death and Life of Great American Cities* (1961), Jane Jacobs objected to all forms of modernist neighborhood planning, arguing instead for mixed-use districts emphasizing street activity. But her critique applied more forcefully to NYCHA "towers in the sky" (e.g., thirteen-story high-rises) than six-story buildings.

link the separation of races enforced in the various NYCHA projects to larger patterns of residential discrimination established in the city during the period.[26] But in terms of their physical design, all the projects sprang from a similar utopian idealism.

Even if the city's future appeared bright, working-class New Yorkers still faced plenty of hardship on an everyday basis. And by no means were the perpetrators of those woes only bankers or exploitative employers on the docks or in the factories. Nor was the Tammany machine the only target of La Guardia's anti-corruption crusade. Throughout his first two terms, La Guardia repeatedly condemned the predatory behavior of the mafia and related syndicates that ruined lives, inflated the prices of all kinds of consumer goods in the city, and enforced their control through intimidation and bloodshed. The theatrical mayor made a show of dumping slot machines in the East River, and throughout his three terms he railed against the gamblers, loan sharks, black marketeers, and "chiselers"[27] who

26 As Richard Rothstein notes in *The Color of Law*, NYCHA adopted an official policy of nondiscrimination in 1939, but it was "nominal" and typically consisted of "a token few other-race families." Richard Rothstein, *The Color of Law: How Our Government Segregated America* (New York: Liveright, 2017), 259.

27 A con artist swindling petty amounts—e.g., borrowing $10 with no intention of paying it back. See *Dictionary of American Slang* (New York: Crowell, 1960). The term was a common insult in the gangster films of the 1930s. La Guardia used it in reference to anyone pilfering small amounts from either individuals or the public till.

preyed on the city's working people. The Italian and Jewish syndicates based in Brownsville had also made inroads in many aboveground economic activities of the era, taking control of industries including waterfront shipping, trucking, garment manufacturing, and baking. A common tactic was protection money shakedown, which shielded business owners from other mobsters. The issue of how to combat mafia violence would be central to La Guardia's next reelection campaign.

CHAPTER TWO:
FLATBUSH AT WAR

In August 1941, as the fall mayoral campaign approached, a new playground opened at Kings Highway and Nostrand Avenue, three blocks from the Sanders family's apartment. As a short item in the *Brooklyn Eagle* noted,[28] it was the 442nd playground built in the city, more than 300 of which had gone up during La Guardia's first two terms. (A list of the New Deal playgrounds shows that they were built in nearly every neighborhood in all five boroughs.[29]) Notably, the *Eagle* item refers to the Nostrand Avenue location as "Flatbush," which is what Bernie Sanders frequently calls the neighborhood that is today considered Midwood.[30]

---

28 *Brooklyn Eagle* (8-9-1941).

29 For list, see: http://kermitproject.org/newdeal/parksprojects.html.

30 For example, as Bernie wrote on his Facebook page in 2017, "I grew up in Flatbush, Brooklyn in a three and a half room rent-controlled apartment and we never had whole lot of money. What I learned then and what I know now is that there [are] decent, hard-working people all across this country who are struggling to get by and want nothing more than to live their lives with dignity." See @berniesanders, Facebook (6-4-2017).

Bernie's older brother Larry recalls that the playground was located on the border between a Jewish area (then considered Flatbush) and an Irish one (Marine Park), creating tensions that resulted in kids of each group throwing rocks at their rivals. The quotidian turf war matched a larger conflict in the city during the period, pitting vocal Irish-Catholic supporters of Hitler against La Guardia and other leading anti-fascists. Larry also remembers that one day when "Bernard" (as he calls him) was about one, girls at the playground urged him to push his little brother as high as he could go on the swing. The end result was the corner of the swing hitting Larry in the head, necessitating stitches. Larry has the scars to this day. The New Deal era left its marks on the Sanders family in many different ways.

On Monday, September 8, 1941—the day Bernie Sanders was born—the city's newspapers announced the beginnings of the Nazi siege of Leningrad. Closer to home, a trial at the Brooklyn Federal Courthouse revealed that a Nazi infiltrator at the Carl I. Norden defense plant in Queens had stolen "America's most prized aviation secret,"[31] the "bomb-sight" technology used for precision

---

31 See *Brooklyn Eagle* (9-8-1941). The infiltrator, Herman Lang, lived in Ridgewood, Queens (then a German-American neighborhood). He and other members of the Ritter spy ring were nabbed because of the work of a German-American double agent, Wilhelm "William" Sebold. See John Strausbaugh, *Victory City: A History of New York and New Yorkers During World War II* (New York: Twelve, 2018), 218–222.

strikes. Meanwhile, New Yorkers and fans of FDR across the nation mourned the passing of the president's mother, Sara Delano Roosevelt, who had died the previous day at the family estate in Hyde Park with her son and Eleanor by her side. Mayor La Guardia, who since May of that year doubled as head of the Roosevelt administration's Office of Civilian Defense, announced that the fuel rationing restrictions enforced in East Coast states over the preceding month would be ending soon. And Brooklyn district attorney Bill O'Dwyer—who had gained fame via his successful prosecutions of ringleaders of the ruthless Brownsville syndicate known as "Murder, Inc."—mapped out his campaign strategy as the Democratic challenger to La Guardia that November. Promising a "constructive and vigorous campaign," O'Dwyer identified the mayor's "shortcomings and dangerous practices," most particularly what he viewed as La Guardia's dubious budget management. In the Irish-born O'Dwyer, Tammany now had a more formidable contender to La Guardia than in the previous two campaigns.[32]

But the movements on battlefields and nuts and bolts of municipal politics were not the only concerns of the day. That evening, Mayor La Guardia would lead the parade of floats at the annual Coney Island Mardi-Gras celebration,

32 Stories drawn from *New York Times* (9-8-41) and *Brooklyn Eagle* (9-8-41). O'Dwyer quoted in latter.

a weeklong late summer fixture for nearly four decades. Photos the next day showed the cheerful Little Flower covered in confetti. Music enthusiasts also had eleven free WPA Music Projects concerts to choose from in Brooklyn parks that week. A group called the Neighborhood Band would perform classical numbers at Prospect Park, swing dance orchestras would play in Williamsburg, and the Negro Melody Singers would appear in both Bed-Stuy and Prospect Park. As the *Eagle* announced, Orson Welles' seminal film *Citizen Kane* would be making its Brooklyn debut later that week. The RKO Albee, a 3,000-seat movie palace in Downtown Brooklyn, would be screening the work "at popular prices" (unlike its "$2 Broadway run!"). Active in both the Federal Theatre Project and the Harlem-based National Negro Theater, Welles drew on the New York City left's perspective in his withering critique of right-wing media mogul William Randolph Hearst. Meanwhile, the movie theater the Sanders family frequented on Nostrand and Kings Highway offered more middlebrow fare, with Abbott and Costello's *In the Navy* lending comedic support to the encroaching U.S. entry into the war.[33]

When the fall mayoral campaign fully kicked off in October, La Guardia contrasted his administration's numerous achievements and dismissed his opponent as

---

33 See *Brooklyn Eagle* (9-8-1941).

simply "the machine candidate." Over the next month he never referred to O'Dwyer by name.[34] At his launch event, the Little Flower reminded his supporters that he and Robert Moses were responsible for "92 new school buildings, 14 health centers, 25 hospital buildings, 325 playgrounds, 6 enclosed markets, 9 child health stations, 845 wading pools for children, 5 major bridges and hundreds of other improvements." He also identified the ethos of his administration as "scientific," a Progressive Era-watchword that stood in opposition to party machine corruption.[35] O'Dwyer did, indeed, have the backing of the city's two most powerful Democratic bosses, Brooklyn's Frank Kelly and Ed Flynn of the Bronx, who was close to FDR and head of the Democratic National Committee. O'Dwyer was also supported by Tammany's leader, Christopher Sullivan, who had fallen out with FDR over the lack of New Deal patronage the organization had received. Along with the Irish party bosses, O'Dwyer positioned himself as an FDR ally (and by the end of the decade he would work quite closely with Eleanor Roosevelt). But there was little doubt which candidate the president supported. La Guardia, as FDR stated at a late October endorsement announcement,

34 *Brooklyn Eagle* (11-5-1941).

35 *New York Times* (10-12-1941).

had run "the most honest, and I believe, the most efficient municipal administration in my recollection."[36]

O'Dwyer, however, mounted a strong challenge. Like his predecessor, he linked La Guardia to Communists—but this time there was more substance to the allegation. Vito Marcantonio, La Guardia's protégé and eventual successor as Congressman from East Harlem, led the Communist-allied wing of the American Labor Party, and the ALP once again backed the mayor.[37] Fully supportive of U.S. entry into the war in the wake of Hitler's invasion of Russia, the CPUSA heartily endorsed La Guardia, a staunch anti-Nazi. Though he also supported the war effort, O'Dwyer nonetheless held appeal for the city's large ranks of Irish supporters of Hitler and Italian sympathizers with Mussolini. Brooklyn was a center of vocal Irish-American support for the Nazis against Ireland's longtime enemy England. That October, Father Edward Curran, a devotee of far-right

---

36 See Williams, 318. While his supporters viewed La Guardia as "efficient," watchdogs warned that his budgeting practices—e.g., borrowing pension funds to balance the 1940–1941 budget, then promising a sales tax cut during a reelection year—posed future danger. See Thomas Kessner, *Fiorello La Guardia and the Making of Modern New York* (New York: Penguin, 1989), 554–558.

37 For Marcantonio's role in the ALP, see Gerald Meyer, *Vito Marcantonio: Radical Politician, 1902–1954* (Albany: SUNY Press, 1989), 25–30. Two Communists were elected to the New York City Council during the period. In 1941, Pete Cacchione took office, representing Brooklyn's Boerum Hill; and in 1943, Harlem's Ben Davis took over the seat vacated by Adam Clayton Powell Jr., who went to Congress. Like Powell, Davis and Cacchione supported La Guardia, but pressured him from the left.

radio priest Father Coughlin, became pastor of St. Joseph, the Brooklyn diocese's large Catholic parish in Prospect Heights; the diocese's newspaper *The Tablet* was also a pro-Nazi organ that carried Coughlin's anti-Semitic rants on its front page. There were outspoken Coughlin supporters in Flatbush during the period as well. In July 1939, *The Nation's* James Weschler provided a rundown of aggressive attempts by the Christian Front—which Weschler described as Irish Catholic Coughlinites drawn from the city's "lower-middle class"—to intimidate the city's Jewish residents. Weschler noted that hawkers sold Coughlin's publication *Social Justice* outside of Erasmus Hall High School in Flatbush. When a teacher named Frances Cohen objected, the Coughlinites called her a Communist and shouted: "Lynch the Jew!"[38] Moreover, the legendary gossip columnist Walter Winchell referred to the Front's ringleader, John Cassidy, as the "Fuhrer of Flatbush."[39] Such hostilities continued in Flatbush through the early years of the war, causing the *Brooklyn Eagle* to editorialize

---

38 James Wechsler, "The Coughlin Terror," *The Nation* (7-22-39).

39 *New York Times* (5-31-95). In 1940, at the behest of FBI director J. Edgar Hoover, federal prosecutors initially charged Cassidy and sixteen other members of the Christian Front with conspiring to overthrow the federal government. Fourteen went to trial. The jury acquitted nine (including Cassidy) and deadlocked on five, who were not retried. Eleven of the seventeen lived in Brooklyn, with Cassidy and four others residing in Flatbush. See *Brooklyn Eagle* (1-15-40).

in a November 1942 headline that the "Outbreak of Anti-Semitism [was] a Disgrace to Brooklyn."[40]

There's no doubt that the Sanders family viewed anyone who supported Hitler with contempt. In 1921, at age 17, Larry and Bernie's father Eliasz Gitman had left Stopnica (in modern-day Poland, near Krakow) and traveled via Belgium to the United States on a passenger ship called the Lapland. In 1927, Gitman became a naturalized U.S. citizen under the name Elias Sanders.[41] At a March 2016 presidential debate (in Flint, Michigan), Sanders stated, "Look, my father's entire family was wiped out by Hitler in the Holocaust." He further recalled going shopping with his mother Dora as a young boy when they would see "people working in stores who had numbers on their arms because they [had been] in Hitler's concentration camp."[42] "Being Jewish," Bernie explained in the mid-1980s, has "greatly influenced my intellectual and emotional development."[43]

---

40 *Brooklyn Eagle* (11-17-1942). Wartime anti-Semitic violence in Flatbush mentioned in Strausbaugh, 155.

41 Hunter Walker, "Bernie Sanders on What He Learned from Brooklyn, Baseball and His Family's Immigrant Roots," *Yahoo News* (9-09-2019). At the time of his naturalization, Eli Sanders—whose occupation was listed as "merchant"—was living at 1672 Broadway, at the edge of Bed-Stuy. For document, see: https://photos.geni.com/p13/27/8e/6a/37/5344483f36af23ae/32126_22580650146353-00954_original.jpg.

42 Daniella Diaz, "Bernie Sanders: My Family Was Wiped Out by Hitler in the Holocaust," CNN.com (3-7-16).

43 Harry Jaffe, *Why Bernie Sanders Matters* (New York: Regan Arts, 2016), 26.

As in many Jewish households during the period, Yiddish was commonly spoken in the Sanders home—and both Larry and Bernie would attend Hebrew School. One fellow Kings Highway area resident told Sanders biographer Harry Jaffe that their neighborhood was "essentially a shtetl."[44] In Bernie's immediate surroundings, Hitler was thus the enemy. Noisy and menacing, the pro-fascist supporters several blocks north in Flatbush were also distinctly in the minority.

For his part, O'Dwyer denounced the Christian Front, a group he had sought to crack down on as district attorney. During the campaign, the mayor and the DA blamed each other for not breaking up the Front's street corner gatherings, of which there had been over one hundred in Brooklyn in the past year.[45] La Guardia's supporters tried to link O'Dwyer to the anti-Semitic agitators, causing the DA's forces to refute that charge. O'Dwyer's primary base of support indeed came from the Democratic Party's mainstream ranks, the leaders of which were anti-fascists.

---

44 Ibid., 27.

45 *Brooklyn Eagle* (1-15-40). During the election year, some questioned whether La Guardia had been tolerating the Christian Front's actions because he gained politically from the hostilities; reflecting on the race two decades later, O'Dwyer repeated that charge. Ronald Bayor, *Neighbors in Conflict: The Irish, Germans, Jews and Italians of New York City, 1929–1941* (Baltimore: John Hopkins University Press, 1978), 140–142. The Front had a sizable contingent in the NYPD, making it difficult for either the mayor or district attorney to crack down. See Wechsler.

Governor Herbert Lehman—FDR's successor and ally, as well as the state's leading Jewish politician—headlined a raucous rally for O'Dwyer at the Brooklyn Academy of Music on the eve of the election. Even as he blasted La Guardia (primarily over the mayor's charge that the state's highest court was doing the governor's bidding), Lehman criticized the undercurrent of anti-Semitic and anti-Italian bigotry in the race.[46] Other prominent New York Democrats spoke out against La Guardia as well. James Farley, FDR's campaign guru and thus the era's political kingmaker, spread word that the president had never offered a cabinet position to the mayor because the Little Flower lacked "gentlemanly instincts," a thinly veiled ethnic smear.[47] In general, Democratic bosses viewed the race as an opportunity to reclaim City Hall. In its endorsement of the borough's district attorney in his bid to become the city's chief executive, the *Brooklyn Eagle* took aim at the incumbent mayor's main line of attack, insisting that O'Dwyer's work prosecuting the mob showed he was "not the tool of any machine."[48]

Sensing a tight race, La Guardia campaigned hard down the stretch. On Monday evening, October 27,

---

46 *Brooklyn Eagle* (11-1-41).

47 Kessner, 498.

48 *Brooklyn Eagle* (11-2-41).

the mayor made two campaign stops in order to rally Brooklyn's Jewish voters. "All are equal as American citizens," he told supporters at a Flatbush synagogue, adding that such a principle "can be accomplished in Europe—but only after we have crushed the Nazi philosophy, the Nazi regime and the Axis powers."[49] He then headed over to the Hotel St. George in Brooklyn Heights, where he addressed an enthusiastic gathering of more than 5,000 Jewish war veterans. In a letter to the editor published three days before the election, *Brooklyn Eagle* reader Harry Weinberger assessed La Guardia's first two terms. In Weinberger's view, the mayor had been "honest and efficient"—and while he had on occasion been "dictatorial" in method, "his purpose at all times has been the betterment of the city and its inhabitants." The letter ended with high praise for Robert Moses. The master builder, Weinberger wrote, had shown the nation "how to make parks, playgrounds and swimming places especially for the coming generation of the United States."[50]

At the eleventh hour, La Guardia—known as a scrappy candidate willing to play dirty, if necessary—sought to undercut O'Dwyer's primary claim to fame. Since taking office as district attorney in 1940, O'Dwyer had initiated

49 *New York Times* (10-28-1941).

50 *Brooklyn Eagle* (11-1-41).

several high-profile prosecutions of the Murder, Inc. hit men who answered to the Brownsville mob bosses Lepke Buchalter and Albert Anastasia. But on the weekend before the election La Guardia released a report that had found widespread jury tampering by the Brooklyn Democratic Party machine—which now stood accused of placing "ringers" in grand juries in order to get connected underworld figures off the hook. The mayor charged that party boss Frank Kelly called the shots in the Brooklyn DA's office, and that Kelly and O'Dwyer had formed "a rotten combination—Politics, Inc. and Crime, Inc."[51] Kelly and his machine counterparts responded by spreading false word that FDR was pulling back his support for La Guardia. On the Monday before Election Day, the president refuted that rumor, stating there was "not one word or vestige of truth" in it.[52]

When the returns rolled in, the Little Flower had garnered a third term, but some bloom had come off the rose. Despite the flurry of grand public works projects built during his second term, the mayor prevailed by only 52–47 percent, dropping eight points from his 1937 margin. La Guardia's winning margin was just over 132,000 votes (with almost the exact same total number of voters—2.2

51 Ibid.

52 *Brooklyn Eagle* (11-3-41).

million[53]—as four years earlier). In Brooklyn, the mayor's tally dropped by 116,000, but he still prevailed by over 90,000 votes, receiving 55 percent of the borough's total ballots. Brooklyn also provided 40 percent of the over 435,000 citywide ALP votes for La Guardia. The Little Flower remained popular in the Sanders family's Midwood district, taking nearly two-thirds of the vote.[54] Across the city, the mayor scored nearly three-quarters of the Jewish vote; but he experienced double-digit drops in his Irish and Italian support. (La Guardia remained popular with black voters.)[55] Four years earlier, La Guardia had received 37 percent of the Irish vote, but now he tallied only 24 percent. That dip can be partially explained by the fact that O'Dwyer was a far stronger candidate than Mahoney, with the former garnering much stronger institutional support. But the pro-Axis sympathies of many Irish and Italian

53 That number is considerably higher than any recent mayoral election in New York City. Over 1.5 million voters cast ballots in Michael Bloomberg's first election in 2001. In the subsequent four races, the total has not reached 1.3 million. Given that the city's total population was 7.4 million in 1940 versus 8.6 million in 2017, the turnout numbers show that the city residents were far more engaged in local politics during the La Guardia era.

54 In Brooklyn's 2nd Assembly District, La Guardia prevailed by 76,000–40,000, again the largest total and widest margin for the mayor in the borough. That differential took on added importance because O'Dwyer won twelve of Brooklyn's twenty-three assembly districts. *Brooklyn Eagle* (11-5-41).

55 In Harlem (then Manhattan's 21st Assembly District), the mayor received just over 70 percent support. In Bed-Stuy, then Brooklyn's 6th Assembly District, La Guardia took in just over 67 percent. *New York Times* (11-5-41) and *Brooklyn Eagle* (11-5-41).

voters were also clearly a factor in trimming the mayor's sails.[56]

In a speech aired by WNYC radio the day after the election, La Guardia looked ahead to his third term. Ominously, he warned:

The next four years are going to be hard, difficult years. Our country is facing a very serious situation, something that appears to have been overlooked during the last few weeks . . . We had a hard time during the past eight years. But to administer this city during the present emergency and perhaps other emergencies—and after this terrible war ends in Europe, to face the after-war condition—is going to require a great deal of thought, work, time, and effort.

Throughout the fourteen-minute address, the feisty mayor railed against the "party bosses" who tried to topple him, praised the "intelligent electorate" that backed him, and "forgave" the voters who went for his opponent. The Little Flower was certainly no shrinking violet. After trashing the "double-crossing" Republican Party leaders in the Bronx and Queens who supported O'Dwyer, La Guardia thanked the American Labor Party for its "unselfish support." This was the second time, he noted, that the ALP—"of which [he was] a member" along with "working men and women"—had given the city a "non-partisan,

---

56 For ethnic vote totals, see Bayor, *Neighbors in Conflict*, 143.

efficient, and honest administration." Rather than take a vacation, the mayor was now "ready to get back to work." La Guardia's passion was palpable. And when he concluded by saying that he had "no interest in the world other than the welfare of the people of my city or the safety of my country," the Little Flower's sincerity was hard to deny.[57]

Despite the dip at the polls, La Guardia remained a popular figure, and his public presence would grow throughout his third term. Sunday, December 7, 1941, is best known as what FDR called "a date which will live in infamy," as a result of Japan's assault on Pearl Harbor. The president delivered that signature line when asking Congress to declare war on Japan, in a live radio speech to the nation the following afternoon. But it was La Guardia who first took to the airwaves late that Sunday afternoon at City Hall. Serving as both mayor of New York City and federal director of the Office of Civilian Defense, La Guardia addressed the city via WNYC, before speaking to the nation live on CBS, NBC, and other national radio networks. He stressed that although Japan's assault—which the mayor blamed on Nazi "thugs and gangsters" steering the Axis nation's war agenda—had occurred in distant Pacific waters, the Eastern seaboard needed to be on high alert. He sought "to assure all persons who have been

57 La Guardia speech, WNYC (11-5-41). See https://www.wnyc.org/story/
mayor-la-guardia-election-returns-speech.

sneering and jeering at defense [preparation] activities . . . that we will protect them now." But the no-nonsense Major also informed that same crowd that "we expect cooperation and there will be no fooling."[58]

That same afternoon, in a move that reflected his anti-Japanese racism, the mayor ordered the NYPD to make sure that all of the city's "Japanese subjects" stayed in their homes "until their status is determined by our federal government." Only 2,000 people of Japanese descent lived in the city; 1,100 had been born in Japan, the rest born in America. But La Guardia—along with FDR, California Attorney General Earl Warren, and other leading figures of the era—saw no distinction between a Japanese national living in the United States and a Japanese American. That stood in contrast to the prevailing views of residents with German and Italian roots shared by the mayor and president.

La Guardia clarified his position regarding the loyalties of the two European groups in a speech four days after Pearl Harbor, on the day Germany and Italy officially declared war on the United States. Speaking from Tacoma, Washington, amid a tour of West Coast defense sites, La Guardia explained to a national radio audience that in his view there was a difference between longtime residents of

58 *New York Times* (12-8-41).

German and Italian descent and "enemy alien subjects," or members of the two nationalities living in America without U.S. citizenship. Among German Americans and Italian Americans, La Guardia averred, "there is but one loyalty—to the United States." Overlooking support from within the two communities for both the Nazis and Mussolini on display in his hometown over the past few years, the mayor declared, "there was not the slightest sentimental or other feeling for the country of their ancestry." To the enemy aliens from the European members of the Axis, La Guardia issued a welcome, albeit one that came with a warning: "There will be no fooling—no monkey business—or we will crack down, and crack down hard."[59]

In a follow-up national radio address ten days later, La Guardia made similar statements about German and Italian nationals residing in the United States, reassuring them that as long as they remained law-abiding, there would "no interference in the normal pursuits of life." After all, he said, neither group was responsible for the actions taken in their home countries—and any mistreatment of them would undermine American principles. But in the words of his leading biographer, "La Guardia pointedly kept the Japanese out of these concerns." The reason he had not

---

59 La Guardia's speech (12-11-1941) was carried on the Mutual Radio Network and aired on WNYC. See https://www.wnyc.org/story/the-problem-of-german-and-italian-nationals-in-the-united-states.

mentioned the Japanese in either radio speech, according to historian Thomas Kessner, was that La Guardia "did not intend for his words to apply to them." Over the next few years, the mayor and former head of the nation's civilian defense fully supported the FDR administration's internment of over 110,000 Americans of Japanese descent. When the West Coast camps began to close in 1944, La Guardia unsuccessfully fought against efforts to relocate several hundred detainees to New York City, then ordered the NYPD to closely surveil their actions once they arrived.[60] A year earlier, after visiting the Gila River internment camp in Arizona, Eleanor Roosevelt had recommended ending the detainment policy; she also rejected the notion that a "Japanese American [is] any more Japanese than a German American is German, or an Italian American is Italian."[61] But neither the president nor the nation's most prominent mayor were as levelheaded as the First Lady, thus leaving a permanent stain on their legacies.

60　Kessner, 536–538. In a letter to La Guardia, leading FDR administration insider Harold Ickes questioned why someone who "had fought long and vigorously for racial equality" would now champion "racial discrimination." Ibid.

61　According to her foremost biographer, Eleanor was "blindsided" by FDR's issuance of Executive Order 9066 in February that initiated the internment camps. Blanche Wiesen Cook, *Eleanor Roosevelt: The War Years and After* (New York: Penguin, 2016), 418. In late April 1943 Eleanor addressed the issue in both her syndicated newspaper column and in an interview with the *Los Angeles Times*. See https://www.nps.gov/articles/erooseveltinternment. htm.

The mayor became a fixture on the airwaves in his
third term. Starting in January 1942, his weekly program
Talk to the People aired on Sunday afternoons on WNYC
(which at that time was owned by the city). The half-
hour show quickly became a popular feature and by the
end of the war claimed two million listeners. The mayor
provided an eclectic mix of updates regarding civilian
defense efforts, condemnations of wartime corruption,
advice in response to listeners' letters, music selections,
recipes, and whatever else was on his mind. And he did
so with his distinctive voice, which sounded like a tenor
saxophone that squeaked. The Little Flower's accent wasn't
specific to one ethnicity but instead a mélange of several.
La Guardia indeed spoke multiple languages—including
English, Yiddish, Italian, and German—and on the program he would read announcements in various tongues.
Combined with the quirky delivery, the mayor's free-form
conversational style provided an aura of intimacy with his
audience. Like so many other New Yorkers of the era, Larry
Sanders distinctly recalls hearing La Guardia passionately
read comic strips on the program during the newspaper
strike of 1945.[62] At the end of one Dick Tracy strip, the
mayor interpreted the moral for young listeners. "Say,

---

62 As longtime *New York Times* reporter Sam Roberts (b. 1947, attended
    Tilden High School in East Flatbush) noted a half-century later, in addition
    to La Guardia airport, the mayor reading comics "provided the most durable
    memory of his mayoralty." *New York Times* (7-30-95).

children, what does it all mean? It means dirty money never brings any luck. No, dirty money always brings sorrow, and sadness, and misery, and disgrace."[63]

As the comic strip example suggested, La Guardia viewed himself as both a leader and a teacher for the city. The local home front during wartime indeed required constant vigilance, causing the mayor to use his platform as a bully pulpit. For example, in a March 1943 broadcast addressing food shortages amid federal government rationing, La Guardia warned:

It is my determination to move speedily and vigorously— right now, in the beginning—against every sort of black marketing within the limits and the power of city government. I also intend to publicize, prosecute, and expose wherever possible every instance of profiteering. It is my belief that if we curb every attempt in the beginning, it will not be long before New York City will be ba-aad medicine and unwelcome territory for black marketeers, trash hogs, profiteers, and chiselers.[64]

The mayor's particular concern that day was the meat sold in the city's butcher shops that had false FDA stamps on it; he vowed to send his administration's health inspectors to investigate suppliers outside the city. Such everyday

---

63 The strike occurred from June 30–July 16, 1945. For newsreel of La Guardia reading the Dick Tracy strip on WNYC, go to https://www.youtube.com/watch?v=GWkOZKPLeo8.

64 La Guardia radio address (3-21-1943), WNYC. See https://www.wnyc.org/story/march-21-1943.

hardships experienced during the war were the central focus of La Guardia's radio program. Having been replaced as director of civilian defense at the outset of 1942, the mayor's radio program allowed him to continue providing essential information and updates regarding his administration's work. The Little Flower's presence in New Yorkers' kitchens and living rooms every Sunday throughout the war was perhaps the most distinctive feature of his third term.

The war took its toll on federal funding for the city, meaning that the mayor's final term saw far fewer public works projects completed than in his first eight years. The WPA ended on June 30, 1943, and a year later, the Public Works Administration (which had funded construction of the Triborough Bridge and Lincoln Tunnel) closed its doors. While major projects like the Brooklyn-Battery Tunnel stalled, one large endeavor did commence: in 1943, construction began on Idlewild Airport (now JFK). For the most part, La Guardia and Moses spent the war years mapping out the future. As promoted to the public, the duo's blueprint included 6,600 acres of parks, sixty new schools, three new hospitals (as well as ten health centers), new buildings at CUNY campuses including Queens College and Brooklyn College, and some of the most controversial highway projects that Moses would later initiate, including the Cross-Bronx Expressway. In early 1943, FDR wrote a letter to La Guardia that conveyed the president's hope that other cities "follow New York's example" in their planning for the aftermath of the war. La Guardia, in turn, enthusiastically read the letter to his WNYC listeners. In the view of the president, the mayor, and the master builder, the New Deal was only on hiatus during the war.[65]

Although the era of public works was far from over, the WPA's demise brought an end to large-scale federal government support for the arts in America. By early 1942, funding for the various WPA cultural initiatives had been redirected to the war effort. Many leading figures from those projects went to work for government agencies, including the Office of War Information. For example, in the middle of the war, actor and director John Houseman, who had been a leading figure in the New York City-based Federal Theater Project, oversaw the Voice of America's vast radio network. The guidebooks remained quite popular for many years. For decades to come, residents of New York State (like their counterparts across the nation) would be reminded of the WPA's efforts each time they went to their local post office. Murals painted by leading artists of the era such as Ben Shahn, whose work titled *The First Amendment* remains on view at the Woodhaven post office in Queens, depicted American history from a left-wing

65 Williams, 373-374.

perspective. Many of the giants of mid-century American arts and letters, from Dorothea Lange and Jackson Pollock to Zora Neale Hurston and Richard Wright, had been sustained by the WPA.

New Deal funding demonstrated the prevailing view of the arts as not simply an elite realm but integral to American life. La Guardia most certainly shared that democratic conception. An enthusiast of classical music, the Little Flower flamboyantly conducted the City Orchestra at Carnegie Hall. (Confident in his abilities, the mayor—and band conductor's son—told the musicians to "just treat me like Toscanini," invoking the legendary Italian conductor.[66]) Musical training, the mayor believed, should be a central component of youth education. So too did FDR, who created the National Youth Administration in 1935. The NYA was under the auspices of the WPA for its first four years, after which it was moved into other agencies before it was finally disbanded in 1943. In addition to funding initiatives for elementary school through graduate students, the NYA provided vocational training and job placement for over four million young men and women aged sixteen to twenty-five.

In April 1942, La Guardia attended the final performance of the city's NYA Orchestra, which was broadcast

66 See Burns, *New York: A Documentary Film*, Episode Six.

on WNYC. Afterwards, the mayor commended the dozen-member ensemble of adolescents for a "splendid concert, so musicianly [sic] performed—I've never heard Tchaikovsky's Fifth better." The Little Flower told the gathering and his radio audience that his "full enjoyment" of the concert was "somewhat marred by the thought that this splendid orchestra is to be discontinued." What followed those statements uniquely encapsuled La Guardia's worldview:

I know of no greater progress or more useful undertaking in the entire social security program of our president than the national youth program. It is the best investment our government has made in many, many years. After all, no one is shocked or complains that the government . . . has spent millions of dollars for the conservation of soil. Can there be any better investment than the conservation, advancement and progress of American music [than the youth orchestra]? It gives every student the opportunity of educational advancement regardless of the economic condition of the family. It is Americanism in its highest terms.

Rather than strictly the federal government's pension program, "social security" was presented by the mayor here in much larger terms. Like FDR and Eleanor, La Guardia held a fundamentally optimistic vision of a future in which the government would actively nourish the soil of American life. Despite his prominent role in the nation's civilian defense, the Little Flower saw no reason to put musical education on hold until after the war. As he insisted:

I don't agree that music is a luxury. And in times of stress, in times of emergency, times of hardship and sorrow—music is a necessity. What is more, we must not permit the war to stop the cultural life of our country.

Few, if any, American politicians have ever made a more forceful declaration in support of the arts.[67]

67 La Guardia radio address, WNYC (4-5-42). See https://www.wnyc.org/story/la-guardia-address-to-members-of-nya-orchestra.

CHAPTER THREE:
ELEANOR'S BROOKLYN

La Guardia was not the only prominent FDR ally in the local headlines during the war. Eleanor Roosevelt's syndicated column had been appearing in the *New York World-Telegram* (a successor to Joseph Pulitzer's *New York World*) six days a week since 1935. Throughout his stint as head of civilian defense in 1941, the mayor worked closely with the First Lady, who served as co-director. Eleanor noted in a postwar memoir that La Guardia had treated her as a secretary and underling, tasking her with opening mail and passing along the projects he wasn't interested in.[68] But at the time of their work together they appeared to the public as partners handling the essential preparations for homefront defense. Throughout the war, Eleanor's popularity

---

68 See Kessner, 500–505. In general, La Guardia was not easy to work with—he liked to be the decision-maker, and often acted impulsively as well as theatrically. That's not an excuse for his sexist treatment of Eleanor, however. In terms of women's equality, FDR—who had hired Frances Perkins and encouraged Eleanor to become her own political entity—was far more progressive than La Guardia.

increased immensely—Larry Sanders recalls that she was a favorite figure of Dora Sanders, his and Bernie's mom. And Dora was by no means the only fan of Eleanor in Brooklyn.

On the second Sunday evening of December 1943, the First Lady visited three armed forces service providers in Brooklyn, located in Bed-Stuy, near the Brooklyn Navy Yard, and in Brooklyn Heights. At each stop, she was greeted by overflow crowds who heard Eleanor issue a resounding call for racial equality. "We will not have peace if we allow prejudice to rule our hearts," she declared, adding that "this thing that we call race prejudice is not only directed against Negroes. I have been getting many letters from soldiers of the Jewish faith and from members of other minority groups who say their rights have been violated." The First Lady gave ribbons to the volunteer staff at the three centers, which provided food to the many soldiers passing through Brooklyn. At the Brooklyn Heights location, which was run by the Teachers Voluntary Service Organization, Eleanor was greeted by more than two hundred people singing "For She's a Jolly Good Fellow." After her talk, a teacher from James Madison High School in Midwood—which Larry and Bernie Sanders would later attend—presented the featured guest with a special gift. Murray Kupferman, Madison's director of arts and crafts, handed Eleanor a hammered silver mug.[69]

69 *Brooklyn Eagle* (12-13-43).

The revered First Lady's partner soon kicked off the election year with one of his most enduring statements. On January 11, 1944, FDR delivered his State of the Union address, albeit this time with a twist. Rather than hold forth before Congress, the president spoke to the nation from the White House, presenting the address on the national radio airwaves as one of his signature "fireside chats." Foreshadowing a fall campaign problem, FDR explained to listeners that he was in ill health—in this case experiencing the flu—and that his doctor had ordered him to stay home. The result was a very short, but extremely powerful State of the Union speech. Even though the war against the Axis powers was far from over, the president began by envisioning a "lasting peace," one that would feature an "American standard of living higher than ever before." But in FDR's view, such a standard encompassed basic social equity. "We cannot be content no matter how high that general standard of living may be," the president declared, "if some fraction of our people—whether it be one-third or one-fifth or one-tenth—is ill-fed, ill-clothed, ill-housed, and insecure." That statement alone is as close to an endorsement of socialism as anything ever to come out of the White House.

FDR's preamble set up the "Second Bill of Rights" that he delineated in the speech. The first ten amendments to the Constitution, the president maintained, had established the "inalienable political rights" that secured

Americans' individual liberty. But in the industrial era, FDR said, "We have come to a clear realization of the fact that true individual freedom cannot exist without economic security and independence." Not addressing the problems of unemployment and resulting consequences like widespread hunger would spur the masses to embrace dictatorship, he warned. Borrowing the signature phrase from the Declaration of Independence, FDR stated that "economic truths have become self-evident." By this he meant "a second Bill of Rights under which a new basis of security and prosperity can be established for all—regardless of station,[70] race or creed." FDR was indeed advocating a radical expansion of the welfare state provisions initiated early in the New Deal. The agenda included:

The right to a useful and remunerative job in the industries or shops or farms or mines of the nation;

The right to earn enough to provide adequate food and clothing and recreation;

The right of every farmer to raise and sell his products at a return which will give him and his family a decent living;

The right of every businessman, large and small, to trade in an atmosphere of freedom from unfair competition and domination by monopolies at home or abroad;

The right of every family to a decent home;

70 A British term for a person's position in a social hierarchy.

The right to adequate medical care and the opportunity to achieve and enjoy good health;

The right to adequate protection from the economic fears of old age, sickness, accident, and unemployment.

The right to a good education.

FDR concluded by vowing to get started with the "implementation" of these new rights immediately after the end of the war. He might have added that, except for the agricultural aspects, the fundamentally egalitarian agenda had begun to be established in New York City over the past decade.

The president's opponent in the fall campaign was New York's Republican governor Thomas Dewey. As Manhattan district attorney in the 1930s, Dewey gained bipartisan support and national fame for his successful prosecutions of both mafia bosses and Tammany Hall leaders. In the 1938 race for governor, Dewey came within two points of unseating FDR's ally Herbert Lehman; four years later, Lehman moved into FDR's administration, and Dewey easily defeated Tammany-backed John J. Bennett Jr., the state's attorney general (who hailed from Brooklyn). In the Sanders family's district, Dewey actually placed third, behind Bennett and Dean Alfange, the ALP's candidate who ran with La Guardia's support.[71] In his first term,

---

71 The ALP's Alfange tallied 10 percent of the statewide total vote (Dewey beat Bennett by 52–36 percent). A Greek political leader, Alfange was an FDR

Dewey governed as a liberal Republican, boosting public sector salaries and amassing a budget surplus earmarked for postwar public works. But in order to appeal to the GOP's national base, Dewey ran as an anti-New Dealer in the 1944 campaign. That positioning contributed to the maneuvers made against left-liberal Henry Wallace, FDR's vice president during his third term, by the Democratic Party leadership. At the July Democratic National Convention in Chicago, party honchos including Ed Flynn from the Bronx led a protracted floor battle that resulted in the replacement of Wallace with Harry Truman, a moderate senator from Missouri.[72] The stakes were particularly high in light of FDR's quickly declining health.[73]

Despite it being a wartime election, Dewey was considered a more viable contender than Wendell Willkie, FDR's

ally and La Guardia threw his support behind his candidacy. The result was that in Midwood, Bennett took home 39,000 votes, Alfange scored 32,000, and Dewey received close to 26,750. Of Alfange's 400,000 total statewide votes, just under 150,000 came from Brooklyn. *Brooklyn Eagle* (11-4-42).

72 Wallace and La Guardia came from the same progressive wing of the Republicans (until Wallace switched parties after joining FDR's administration as Secretary of Agriculture in 1933). The mayor helped lead a public campaign to make Wallace VP in 1940 (see Mason, 294–295), but he didn't play an active role in the 1944 selection process. After Truman emerged victorious, La Guardia said Wallace was defeated by "his friends, not by his opponents," referring to the latter's superior maneuvering on the convention floor. Everything "will be all right," he added. *New York Times* (7-23-44).

73 Just before the DNC, a team of leading doctors examined the president, and one accurately predicted that FDR would not be able to survive through his entire fourth term. See Jeff Greenfield, "The Year the Veepstakes Really Mattered," *Politico Magazine* (July 2016).

challenger four years earlier. The Roosevelts were determined not to lose their home state, thus bringing both the
president and the First Lady to the county with the most
Democratic votes. In late September, Eleanor headlined
a women's voter registration rally in Brownsville. While
a crowd of 2,000 packed the Loew's Parkway Theatre,
the *Brooklyn Eagle* estimated that 1,500 more fans gathered outside. The First Lady called the United States "the
hope of the world," expressing her vision that American
democracy would set an example for other nations to
"govern themselves and do it successfully." Three female
Jewish leaders from Brownsville also took the stage. In late
October, Eleanor (along with the family dog, Fala) and La
Guardia accompanied FDR on a twenty-mile motorcade
through Brooklyn. The *Eagle* reported that the "largest
crowds greeting the president were in Brownsville, where
all along Pitkin Avenue people stood six or seven deep at
the curb," including an elderly man holding a makeshift
sign reading "F.D.R.—our Messiah." Like La Guardia, the
Roosevelts were clearly held in high esteem by Brooklyn's
large Jewish community.[74]

In addition to the Brooklyn Army Terminal and the
Brooklyn Navy Yard, FDR's motorcade brought him to one
of the borough's most iconic destinations, Ebbets Field.

74 *Brooklyn Eagle* (9-29-1944) and (10-22-1944).

Located on Bedford Avenue in what was then considered the northern end of Flatbush (now Crown Heights), the ballpark was home to the Brooklyn Dodgers. It was cold and rainy that Saturday morning, diminishing the anticipated attendance of 45,000. But 15,000 diehard fans nevertheless turned out to cheer the president. Just before the motorcade arrived, the crowd—which had been chanting "We Want Roosevelt!"—was listening to a rendition of the hit song "Oh, What A Beautiful Morning." But as the entourage made its way through the center-field fence, the band struck up "Hail To The Chief."[75] Mayor La Guardia joined FDR and New York senator Robert Wagner on the platform. The president explained that he was there to support his close ally Wagner, who was running for reelection against Dewey's candidate Thomas Curran. FDR then informed his supporters that he "had to make a terrible confession to you":

I come from the state of New York, and I practice law in New York City, but I have never been in Ebbets Field before. [Loud cheers from the crowd and laughter from FDR]. *I've rooted for the Dodgers.* [Even louder cheers.] *And I'll come back here and see 'em play.* [Loudest cheers of all.][76]

75 *Brooklyn Eagle* (10-22-1944).

76 See clip from PBS documentary *The Roosevelts* (2014): https://www.pbs.org/video/roosevelts-fdr-visits-ebbits-field/.

FDR was then helped back into his car, where he rejoined Eleanor and waved his hat to the grandstands on his way out. He never would return to see the Dodgers play.

The *New York Post* and *Brooklyn Eagle* presented a sampling of the Ebbets Field crowd's support that illustrated the diversity of FDR's coalition. Joseph Weissman, a fifty-eight-year-old shoemaker and poet from East New York, was the first person in line that morning, having arrived at 5 a.m. Three hours later, Peter Djerejian left his night-shift job as a machinist at the Navy Yard, explaining that his wife told him "not to come home" before heading to the ballpark to salute Roosevelt. Dignitaries at the event included Justice Juvenal Marchisio, president of American Relief for Italy, and Lt. Elaine Karg, the only black doctor in the Dutch Army. "This is the first time the president has been in Ebbets Field," exclaimed the ballpark's chief usher Johnny Haines, adding, "I am excited! Holy smokes!" Fort Hamilton High School student Frank Inciardi observed that while he couldn't vote, FDR was "my president, too." While eleven-year-old Judy Resnikoff sported two FDR buttons, the largest pro-Roosevelt button was reportedly worn by seventeen-year-old David Silverberg from Sheepshead Bay. As the surnames suggest, a cross-section of Brooklyn's mostly non-Irish ethnic white working class turned out to show support for FDR. But the president also could count on black support as well. An unidentified

NYPD captain (presumably Irish) received cheers from spectators who saw him escort what the *Eagle* described as an "aged Negro woman" down to a front-row seat. "This is what my boy is fighting for overseas," the captain said as he received pats on the back from fans in the stands.[77]

The results of the November election showed that FDR's visit to Brooklyn had paid dividends. Although the president won a fourth term by a comfortable national margin (53–46 percent), Dewey carried a dozen states. FDR's five-point margin of victory in New York stemmed mainly from his support in Manhattan and Brooklyn. The president garnered over 750,000 votes in Kings County, defeating Dewey by nearly 365,000—and statewide, just over 310,000 votes separated the two candidates. Roughly 35 percent of FDR's nearly 500,000 votes on the ALP line came from Brooklyn. (En route to reelection, Wagner received approximately 20,000 more Kings County votes than the president). There was no disputing who the preferred candidate was in the Sanders family's district. FDR carried Midwood by nearly 50,000 votes, including two from the Sanders household. Buoyed by its Brooklyn support, the Roosevelt coalition now looked forward to a fourth term.

---

77 *New York Post* (10-22-1944) and *Brooklyn Eagle* (10-22-44).

Six days after the election, Eleanor Roosevelt came back to the borough, this time to address supporters at Brooklyn College. It was the second public appearance by the First Lady after the campaign. Located on Bedford Avenue in Midwood, Brooklyn's flagship CUNY campus had been built with New Deal funding. La Guardia attended the ground-breaking ceremony in 1935, and on the eve of the 1936 election, the mayor returned to welcome FDR, who laid the cornerstone of the gym. On November 13, 1944, more than five thousand co-ed students filled the campus quad on a sunny autumn afternoon to see the First Lady, who reiterated her familiar message about the need for inter-racial "unity." Eleanor recounted her experiences visiting troops in Hawaii and Guadalcanal, explaining that she had seen white and black soldiers receive equal treatment (albeit in separate units). She also noted that Jewish, Catholic, and Protestant soldiers had fought side-by-side and attended each other's funerals. Given the fight against intolerance in the war effort, the First Lady said, "we must be more considerate of it" in peace.[78]Although her days in the White House were numbered, Eleanor would remain a forceful advocate of equality in the postwar period.

In early January 1945, FDR delivered his final State of the Union. Presented to Congress on the first Saturday

78 *Brooklyn Eagle* (11-14-44).

of the new year, the speech is not considered as influential as the "Four Freedoms" or "Second Bill of Rights" but the final address laid out a blueprint for the postwar—and post-FDR—era that remains important. It was significantly longer than the previous year's speech, although the first two-thirds of it were devoted to pressing concerns on the various battlefronts overseas. When he returned to the home front, FDR picked up on the Second Bill of Rights he had advocated a year earlier. He focused on the first item on that list, calling "the right to a useful and remunerative job" the "most fundamental" of the new rights, because the "fulfillment of others in large degree depends on it." At the same time, the president said, the provision of other items on the list—housing, education, medical care, etc.—would require the creation of jobs. FDR envisioned the extension of the wartime full employment economy into the aftermath of the war. The president declared:

Our policy is, of course, to rely as much as possible on private enterprise to provide jobs. But the American people will not accept mass unemployment or mere makeshift work. There will be need for the work of everyone willing and able to work—and that means close to 60,000,000 jobs.

Full employment means not only jobs—but productive jobs. Americans do not regard jobs that pay substandard wages as productive jobs.

The standard of a productive job FDR shared with the nation's working people was in sync with the industrial era. During the war many of the nation's leading manufacturing sites—including the Brooklyn Navy Yard—operated twenty-four hours per day in three shifts. In FDR's estimation, once the hostilities abroad subsided, the productivity at home would continue.

What FDR envisioned was not socialism but more akin to social democracy, although he didn't use either term. Rather than nationalize the steel, automobile, or financial industries, FDR wanted the federal government to oversee them via regulation. In his words, "We must make sure that private enterprise works as it is supposed to work— on the basis of initiative and vigorous competition, without the stifling presence of monopolies or cartels." The federal government, FDR said, must assist "private capital" in making large-scale investments that expanded the nation's industrial capacity. Keynesian deficit spending would continue to support major public works projects. The president said that there would be federal money for "thousands of airports" and an "overhaul [of] our national highway system." Whether constructing a large-scale project used by the general public or a single-family home, Roosevelt's blueprint required unity among many actors. "To make a frontal attack on the problems of housing and urban reconstruction," the president stated, "will require thoroughgoing cooperation between industry and labor, and the federal, state, and local governments." The postwar era would witness various iterations of many items on FDR's agenda. But the disparate parts were never assembled into the whole.

As FDR's final term began, the end of the war appeared on the horizon. By the end of January 1945, Allied forces had won the Battle of the Bulge. In early February, FDR then met with Churchill and Stalin for the landmark conference at Yalta. But as he and his powerful counterparts outlined a new political map for postwar Europe, it became increasingly evident that the gaunt, pale FDR would not be around to see it enacted. Even as rumors of his ill-health swirled, the president's demise was still unexpected. On Thursday, April 12, Roosevelt was at the "Little White House" in Warm Springs, Georgia, a destination he had frequented over the preceding two decades because the warm baths helped relieve the pain of his paralytic illness (then diagnosed as polio). While that condition was common knowledge, it was a cerebral stroke that caused FDR's death at 4:35 that Thursday afternoon. At 5:48 p.m., the White House announced the president's passing, and within two hours Harry Truman had taken the oath of office. At only sixty-three, FDR was younger at the time of his death than the first seven U.S. presidents.

News of FDR's passing came to Mayor La Guardia when he was presiding over an early evening ceremony for WNYC. The mayor had gathered at the Plaza Hotel with Manhattan borough president Edgar Nathan and several other elected officials to present an award (for "patriotic service") from the Sons of the American Revolution to the municipal radio station. Just over twenty minutes after the White House announced FDR's death, a grief-stricken mayor waxed poetic in a ten-minute address carried by WNYC. "The shock and sorrow are so great," the Little Flower intoned, but "we must carry on—because of him, whose death the entire world mourns." In the room with him, the mayor said, were "men of different ancestry, of different religious faith, [and] of different political beliefs . . . yet [now] we've also seemed to have been brought closer together." But, as the mayor noted, FDR was held in the highest esteem not only by the dignitaries that surrounded him at the Plaza. Indeed, for working people in the city and across the land, Roosevelt's presidency had delivered "hope—for the future of their children, and [for] their grandchildren." The mayor's message no doubt rang true in the living rooms of Brooklyn.

Suddenly, La Guardia shifted gears. Invoking his own "Roman ancestry," he declared, "we must buck up!" The Major now barked out commands. "Every American has a responsibility—and a duty—to carry on . . . as he would have us carry on." La Guardia declared that "no matter how humble," Americans needed "to insist that [FDR's] ideals were translated into reality and into everyday life." With the bombast of a histrionic Shakespearean actor, the Major declared that those ideals included:

A better world for all! Economic security for the impoverished people of impoverished countries of this world. For permanent peace! My friends, this could not just have happened. There must be some reason for it all . . . Is it that this sorrow must emphasize into us that responsibility and that unselfishness so necessary to bring about a happier world?

The tributes had only just begun. Under the full-spread headline "The Man Whose Courage Overcame Disaster . . . to Lead History's Greatest Fight for Freedom," the next day's *New York Post* ran a two-page photo retrospective of FDR's life. The same edition of the tabloid carried a nearly full-page editorial assessing the president's legacy (with a full-page photo of FDR on the adjacent page). Exhorting readers to "rise" from the collective "desolation," the *Post* declared that "we are simultaneously in sight of world peace, in sight of world security, in sight of 60,000,000 jobs, enough for all Americans—his goals." Many stores, movie theaters, and offices across the city closed on Friday afternoon to observe the White House memorial service. That Saturday, La Guardia and his fellow New Yorkers saluted the fallen president in a funeral procession and

City Hall ceremony. Both the mayor and his city had most
certainly lost a good friend and ally. The new reality was
immediately clear to La Guardia, given his frosty relationship with now-President Truman. But as he had insisted
in the spur of the moment at the Plaza Hotel, "Franklin D.
Roosevelt is not dead. His ideals live . . . I call upon all New
Yorkers to carry on."[79]

79 La Guardia address, WNYC (4-12-1945). See: https://www.wnyc.org/series/
fiorello-h-la-guardia/archival-audio/1. *New York Post* and *New York Times*
(4-13-1945 and 4-14-1945).

CHAPTER FOUR:
FIORELLO'S FAREWELL

Given that he was up for reelection that fall, La Guardia also needed to reckon with his own political future. He faced the prospect of managing a fourth term without his most powerful ally. After twelve years as the central figure in New York City politics, La Guardia now had an array of enemies beyond simply the Tammany and Democratic machine bosses.[80] The Major's combative, autocratic style wore down many of the liberal Republican Party stalwarts who initially backed him. Black leaders, including Harlem's Adam Clayton Powell Jr. and Ben Davis, were sharply critical of La Guardia's inaction in the wake of the Harlem Riot of 1943; and throughout the mayor's third term, housing discrimination became a heated issue from the proposed Stuyvesant Town development to redlined

---

80 Like his successors Ed Koch (1978–1989) and Michael Bloomberg (2002–2013), La Guardia also confronted the reality that New York City's restive voters grow weary of any figure who stays in a powerful office for too long. That tendency applied less to FDR primarily because of the war effort.

Bed-Stuy.[81] O'Dwyer, meanwhile, promised to be an even more formidable contender this time around. In June 1942, O'Dwyer took leave from the Brooklyn district attorney's office to serve in the army, eventually becoming a decorated brigadier general on the Italian front. Weary from twelve years of his famously non-stop daily routine,[82] La Guardia decided it was time to step away from City Hall.

On the first Sunday of May 1945, the Little Flower broke the news on his WNYC broadcast, which was now estimated to reach as many as two million listeners. "[T]here is always the danger of becoming a bit stale in office," he noted candidly. Though term limits did not exist for either the president or New York City mayor, La Guardia indeed made the case for them. Echoing Thomas Jefferson, the Little Flower declared that "I do not believe, in our form of government, chief executives should be elected time after time . . . [r]otation in office is good [and]

---

81   Kessner, 528–536 and 555–560.

82   In February 1945, the popular journalist John Gunther spent a full day at City Hall with the mayor. Gunther's time-stamped chronology became a notable chapter (titled "The Not-So-Little Flower") in his 1947 bestseller *Inside U.S.A.* As recorded by Gunther, a day in the life of La Guardia was a whirlwind of phone calls, meetings with commissioners as well as average city residents (e.g., a delegation of butchers at City Hall to discuss the meat shortage), planning sessions about current projects (e.g., Idlewild airport), and monitoring of gambling and other underworld activity. After parting ways with the mayor at 8 p.m., Gunther concluded that it was "one of the most remarkable—and remarkably full—days I've ever gone through. [And] Fiorello H. La Guardia is one of the most remarkable, most useful, and most stimulating men American public life has ever known." Gunther, chapter 34.

necessary in a democracy." The mayor acknowledged that he had supported FDR's third and fourth campaigns but chalked that up to the war effort (while La Guardia said nothing about his own third run, the rationale was surely the same). Rather than remind listeners of the many landmark achievements the city had seen over the past eleven and a half years, the Little Flower emphasized the integrity of his administration. After ticking off the names of several commissioners (including Moses), the mayor declared that under his watch there had been "no fixing, graft, favoritism, or stealing." With no shortage of pride, La Guardia pronounced that his tenure had produced "a new model of intelligent, clean, scientific, non-political municipal government." And just as the mayor had advised when FDR passed away a month earlier, it was now up to everyday New Yorkers to "carry on."[83]

Although the mayor still had over a half year to go in office, the tributes quickly poured in. James Hagerty, then City Hall reporter for the *New York Times* (and later White House press secretary under Eisenhower), issued a particularly glowing appraisal. Hagerty insisted that La Guardia was "The David who slew the Tammany Goliath, this little figure of a reformer who gave the city the good government and who did it during the black years of

83 La Guardia radio address, WNYC (5-6-1945). See https://www.wnyc.org/
    story/may-6-1945. Transcript in *New York Times* (5-7-1945).

depression and war." In the reporter's view, the mayor's "terrific personal drive and his whiplash tongue" were keys to his success. But it wasn't just style or his managerial approach that set the mayor apart. It was the fact that La Guardia had delivered the goods. As Hagerty noted:

He had built bridges, fine public buildings, extensive parkways and subways. He had helped clear slums and provide low-cost public housing, parks and playgrounds. He was the one who got great, modern hospitals and airports. The people of the city thought of him as a friend of labor yet did all he could for business.

La Guardia's record of achievement during his tenure in office far surpasses that of any New York City mayor who has succeeded him.

The mayor's early May announcement that he would not run again coincided with the end of the war in Europe. At the end of April, Mussolini had been killed—and two days later, Hitler committed suicide. On the Monday after the mayor's radio broadcast, the Axis powers in Europe declared an unconditional surrender. But the war continued in the Pacific through early August, when President Truman made his fateful decision to drop the atomic bombs on Hiroshima and Nagasaki. With Japan's surrender on September 2, World War II had come to an end. Yet as the fall campaign to replace La Guardia took shape, the city soon witnessed a preview of the new battlefields on the home front. In late September, 15,000 building service workers—led by elevator operators—went out on strike, shutting down Manhattan's main business districts. On October 1, the city's longshoremen followed suit, bringing much of the city's port traffic in both Manhattan and Brooklyn to a standstill over the next two weeks.[84] Although City Hall was not responsible for private-sector labor relations, no long-time incumbent mayor (let alone one close to labor movement radicals) would have fared well amid the volatility. In bowing out, La Guardia surely had made the right choice.

Bill O'Dwyer was the clear front-runner among three leading candidates on the November ballot. The city's Republican leaders had tapped a loyal machine Democrat, Judge Jonah Goldstein, to run on their line. In 1944 the ALP had splintered, with the anti-Communist wing (led by garment workers union head David Dubinsky) forming the Liberal Party. La Guardia's longtime ally Vito Marcantonio remained in control of the ALP. The Liberal Party supported Goldstein, while the ALP backed O'Dwyer. Not a fan of Republican bosses, Dubinsky's new party, or Tammany judges, La Guardia clearly couldn't support Goldstein. But O'Dwyer's ties to the Democratic Party bosses also made it

84 For further details on the postwar strike wave, see Joshua B. Freeman, *Working-Class New York: Life and Labor Since World War II* (New York: New Press, 2000), 3–6.

impossible for the Little Flower to support him. La Guardia thus threw his weight behind Newbold Morris, then City Council president. Morris shared the outgoing mayor's ethical standards but was no match in terms of charisma—the Little Flower once noted that his preferred successor spoke like a Boy Scout. The theatrical figure somehow thought that placing Morris on a line called "No Deal Party" (referring to the candidate's independence from party bosses) would capture voters' imaginations. In the homestretch of the campaign, La Guardia gave frequent radio addresses in support of Morris.

Eleanor Roosevelt, meanwhile, served as one of O'Dwyer's most vocal champions. In bestowing her blessing on O'Dwyer in late September, the former First Lady assured voters that "General O'Dwyer can be supported by those in the Democratic ranks who want good government in the city of New York." Driving home her point that O'Dwyer was not simply the pick of the party machine, as well as highlighting her own independence, Eleanor asserted that "I would not campaign for anyone who was just a Democrat."[85] On Sunday, October 14, the *Brooklyn Eagle*'s lead story reported that a borough-wide straw poll showed O'Dwyer crushing Goldstein by two-to-one, with Morris barely reaching 5 percent. The same

85 *New York Times* (9-30-1945).

edition included mention that the former First Lady would headline a reception that Monday on behalf of O'Dwyer at the Hotel St. George in Brooklyn Heights. Four thousand women were expected to attend. Eleanor also returned to the borough twice in late October, once for a commissioning ceremony (attended by President Truman, among many other dignitaries) of the USS *Franklin D. Roosevelt* at the Navy Yard; a few days later, she came back to the Loew's Theatre in Brownsville, this time to buy a Victory War Bond from the Hollywood actress Greer Garson. Although neither event was an O'Dwyer rally, the visits by the revered Roosevelt certainly didn't hurt the Democratic contender's chances.[86]

O'Dwyer positioned himself as a resolute New Dealer, pledging to carry out the blueprint for the war's aftermath that La Guardia and Moses had laid out two years earlier. In its ringing endorsement, the *Brooklyn Eagle* highlighted the fact that O'Dwyer had promised "to retain Bob Moses as the city's vast public works program."[87] Backed by New York's entire Democratic establishment—and facing two drab candidates who cut into each other's vote—"General" O'Dwyer marched to an unsurprising landslide victory in November, winning by nearly 700,000 votes, including

---

86 *Brooklyn Eagle* (10-14-1945, 10-27-1945 and 10-29-1945).

87 *Brooklyn Eagle* (11-4-1945).

57 percent support in Brooklyn. As the *Eagle* noted on its front-page recap, the only surprise was that Newbold Morris, "protégé of Mayor La Guardia," finished less than 25,000 vote tallies behind the Republican contender Goldstein, a clear sign of La Guardia's political muscle. The Sanders family's Midwood district provided Morris with his largest total in Brooklyn.[88]

While New York's Democratic leaders celebrated their re-conquest of City Hall, questions surrounded La Guardia's election maneuvering as well as the legacy he would leave behind. Did he really intend to help O'Dwyer by undercutting the Republican candidate? If the Little Flower dreaded the return of the machine bosses, why not unify the opposition? And now that Tammany and company were again ascendant, could La Guardia really claim to have eradicated machine rule? As critics charged throughout his twelve-year reign, the Little Flower's autocratic style and clashes with party bosses meant that despite his popularity, there was no semblance of a La Guardia movement. As seen by his support for Morris, a candidate he chose by default, the mayor had not groomed a successor. While the Major was a resolute foe of corruption, there was certainly no guarantee—the claims of Eleanor and other powerful supporters notwithstanding—that General O'Dwyer

88 *Brooklyn Eagle* (11-7-1945).

would follow suit. Indeed, as the outgoing mayor left City Hall, it seemed quite possible that La Guardia's standard of "honest efficient municipal government" would be a thing of the past.

In his final broadcast on WNYC, La Guardia clarified his intention to remain an active presence in the city's political conversation. O'Dwyer would take office two days later—on January 1, 1946—but the Little Flower announced that he'd be back on the air the following Sunday, with two new programs on ABC radio. The New York City affiliate (then WJZ) would air his half-hour discussion of local politics on early Sunday afternoon, and ABC's national network would carry La Guardia's thirty-minute overview of national affairs on Sunday evenings.[89] The Little Flower further advised that he would be writing two weekly columns, one to appear in *PM*, the city's left-leaning daily newspaper (then edited by James Weschler, formerly of *The Nation*). La Guardia's other installment would be sponsored by Sachs, a furniture company, and it would run in several papers, including William Randolph Hearst's *New York Journal-American* and the *New York Post*, then a liberal outlet owned by Dorothy Schiff. The multiple platforms promised to allow the mayor to continue settling scores

---

89 Many radio shows had corporate sponsors at the time. June Dairy Products, which made a popular item called Blue Moon Cheese, backed La Guardia's local program. *Liberty* magazine, a more literary rival of the *Saturday Evening Post*, sponsored his national show. *New York Times* (12-31-45).

with his critics, as well as deliver his familiar blend of political insights, music reviews, and advice to his fans.

But as he prepared to turn over the keys to City Hall to O'Dwyer, La Guardia also fretted about the future of the most important project of his final term. One week earlier, the City Council had eliminated $45 million that the city's capital budget earmarked for the Idlewild project. O'Dwyer had signaled his support for the move, which was perceived as a slap in the face to La Guardia. "I am going to appeal to [O'Dwyer] again," the Little Flower informed his WNYC listeners, "about the great mistake and the great damage to our city in scuttling Idlewild Airport." Robert Moses would soon negotiate a new revenue stream for the project, and he would oversee many of the other initiatives La Guardia highlighted in his final broadcast as mayor. At the top of La Guardia's list was an expansion of the city's already sizable library system. In a number of areas, including the Sanders family's Brooklyn neighborhood, the city was renting space in makeshift locations. The Little Flower expressed hope that the new branch locations he and the city planning commission had called for would come to fruition. More ominously, La Guardia also urged listeners to obtain a map that the commission had put out featuring the new highways Moses envisioned for the city. After reading a prayer by Transcendentalist poet Theodore

Parker, La Guardia signed off as mayor with his signature phrase, "Patience and fortitude."[90]

Although he remained a continued presence in city affairs after he left office, La Guardia was not able to use his popularity to play the role of kingmaker. That's largely because the Little Flower was not willing to back candidates simply based on their electability. His renewed alliance with the left led him to support radical challengers to the preferred candidates of the city's Democratic and Republican machines, the bosses of which the Major continued to despise. In February 1946, La Guardia endorsed the ALP's candidate Johannes Steel in what the *New York Times* later described as a "bitterly contested" election for a seat in Congress representing Manhattan's Lower East Side. Steel, foreign news editor of the *New York Post*, was closely allied with the CPUSA. La Guardia was thus throwing his weight behind Vito Marcantonio and the Communist-aligned ALP's insurgent challenger to incumbent Democrat Arthur G. Klein, a nonentity machine politician but a reliable FDR supporter in Congress. La Guardia's backing of Steel was unsuccessful, as Klein narrowly prevailed (by less than four thousand votes). But it

90 La Guardia radio address (12-30-1945). See https://www.wnyc.org/story/laguardia-fiorello-h-talk-to-the-people-last-broadcast, and *New York Times* (12-31-1945).

also illustrated that the former mayor's core convictions—anti-machine and left-affiliated—remained as strong as ever.[91]

In addition to monitoring the local scene, La Guardia's newspaper columns and radio broadcasts[92] kept a close eye on postwar reconstruction at home and abroad. The former mayor's advocacy on behalf of the United Nations' program of food distribution to war-torn nations led President Truman to appoint La Guardia as director general of the UN's Relief and Rehabilitation Administration in March 1946. This made the Major an international goodwill ambassador who traveled throughout Europe, receiving a hero's welcome in Rome. In Germany La Guardia minced no words in attacking the U.S. military's rapprochement with Nazi "brutes" and "rascals"—and he called for the U.S. to welcome as many as 150,000 Jewish refugees. Two years before Congress passed the Marshall Plan that funded European reconstruction efforts, New York's former mayor advocated a "worldwide WPA."

---

91 *New York Times* (2-15-1946 and 12-3-1988). In its 1988 obituary, the *Times* noted that Steel had fled Germany after Hitler was elected and soon became one of the Fuhrer's most vocal critics in the pages of the *New York Post*.

92 La Guardia's splenetic attacks on his foes (e.g., calling Joseph Medill Patterson, the conservative publisher of the *Daily News*, a Nazi sympathizer) caused some local newspapers to drop his syndicated column after only a few weeks. He also lost sponsorship for the national radio broadcast within two months, because he criticized his sponsor *Liberty* magazine's advertisers. See Kessner, 579.

Despite his UN appointment by Truman, the Little Flower became a vocal critic of the president's initial escalations of the Cold War. Along with Henry Wallace, Truman's first Secretary of Commerce, La Guardia advocated cooperation with the Soviet Union. In July 1946, Wallace was forced to resign after he warned presciently that Truman was initiating a never-ending arms race. La Guardia boldly defended Wallace, calling him "a casualty of peace." The Little Flower, in turn, became a casualty of the Cold War when he was essentially pushed out of his UN position by the Truman administration at the end of 1946.[93]

Other than Wallace and La Guardia, there were few prominent critics of the Cold War as it took shape under Truman, making the Little Flower's passing in 1947 an even greater loss. Through his final nine months, even as he was in and out of the hospital dealing with what turned out to be pancreatic cancer, the former mayor valiantly made the case on the airwaves and in print for improved relations with the USSR. Turning to the home front, La Guardia advocated for national health insurance and greater unemployment protections for workers laid off by automation. Unlike the Truman administration, which continued the New Deal but embraced the Cold War, the

93 Truman's State Department viewed the food relief program as too
    sympathetic to pro-Soviet governments. Despite La Guardia's pleas,
    funding for it was not renewed at the end of 1946. Ibid., 579–588.

Little Flower adhered to FDR's vision of a cooperative post-war world that carried on the New Deal. But on Tuesday, September 16, La Guardia fell into a coma, then died four days later. He was only sixty-four.

The cover of the late Saturday edition of the *New York Post* featured a photo of La Guardia working at his desk as mayor. No one could deny the Little Flower's commitment to building a better city. As the *Post*'s two-page bio concluded, the six-term congressman and three-term mayor "wanted to go down in history as a liberal who fought for the ordinary man and woman and particularly for their children. He undoubtedly will." Similar tributes poured in, including many from various figures that La Guardia had clashed with over the years. He was "incorruptible as the sun," declared President Truman, adding that the Little Flower was "a fearless fighter who gave no quarter when he thought that righteousness and the public interest were on his side." Mayor O'Dwyer saluted his predecessor's "unselfish devotion to the people and his untiring and energetic efforts to promote public welfare." James Farley and Ed Flynn, two of the key Democratic leaders who tried to dislodge La Guardia from City Hall in 1941, now offered their respects. Many of the Little Flower's allies also chimed in. "First Roosevelt, now Fiorello," lamented Henry Wallace, who viewed the two figures as "taken from us when we need them most—but the fight must go on."

Hyman Blumberg, state chair of the American Labor Party, summed up the view of many union leaders in bidding farewell to the man he called "labor's greatest friend." In her "My Day" column in Monday's *World-Telegram* (syndicated nationally), Eleanor Roosevelt was notably candid. La Guardia, she wrote, "had a decided unevenness of temperament," and recalling their days working together, she said that the Little Flower lacked the ability to "delegate his authority." Even so, Eleanor stated, La Guardia was "good for his country," for he "loved it as he loved his children."[94]

Ordinary New Yorkers also partook in the tributes. On Sunday, September 21, 45,000 people journeyed to the Cathedral of St. John the Divine, the Episcopal diocese in Manhattan's Morningside Heights, to see the Little Flower one last time. Monday's edition of the *New York Post* carried photos of the mourners. One caption described a middle-aged woman who was "visibly shaken, after peering at [the] body of the Little Flower"; another said the "sight of her friend and champion brings handkerchief to the quivering face of [an] elderly woman." Another photo showed a middle-aged white couple holding two young black boys staring into the coffin, with the caption suggesting that the children were "memorizing the features of the man who will go down in history as the city's greatest mayor."

94 *New York Post* (9-20-1947). Tributes in *New York Times* (9-21-1947). Roosevelt column in *New York World-Telegram* (9-22-1947).

Nearly 4,000 devotees attended the next day's funeral, and according to the *New York Times*, another 2,500 mourners milled outside the cathedral. Seats had been reserved for what the paper referred to as 1,000 "notables," meaning that most attendees were everyday working-class fans of the fallen mayor. Despite rain that morning, 500 enthusiasts had arrived at 7 a.m. for the afternoon service. During the ceremony the common folks stood with dignitaries including Governor Dewey, Mayor O'Dwyer, and business tycoon John D. Rockefeller Jr. to sing one of the Little Flower's favorite hymns, "For All the Saints Who From Their Labors Rest."[95]

In his radio broadcasts over the preceding six years, the bandleader's son had provided suggestions for the playlist heard at his funeral. As La Guardia's coffin was placed in a hearse outside St. John the Divine, an ensemble made up of members of the city's police, fire, and sanitation departments performed Chopin's funeral march. La Guardia was then buried at Woodlawn Cemetery in the Bronx, the resting place of Herman Melville, pioneering journalist Nellie Bly, and Harlem Renaissance poet Countee Cullen (and later Robert Moses, Duke Ellington, and Miles Davis). The music-loving mayor no doubt would have most appreciated the special concert presented in his honor the following Sunday at the Brooklyn Museum. Members of the American Federation of Musicians union assembled a one-hundred-piece orchestra to perform Bach's "Come, Sweet Death," Wagner's funeral march, and Beethoven's Fifth Symphony. Broadcast live on WNYC, the solemn concert captured the sense of loss shared by the many thousands of ordinary New Yorkers who viewed La Guardia not only as a genuinely devoted public servant but also as a member of their family.[96]

After FDR's death two years earlier, the Little Flower had implored city residents to "carry on." Roosevelt's local coalition would indeed remain intact for the next several decades, during which time there was bipartisan support in New York for New Deal-style public works and social spending. Except for the radical left and his elite Republican backers, La Guardia's base would quickly return to the local Democratic fold. That he left behind no semblance of his own political machine meant that the mayor's three-term reign was ultimately a momentary rupture in New York City's political landscape. But La Guardia's seismic impact on the city's physical landscape would endure.

96 *New York Times* (9-26-1947).

PART TWO

CHAPTER FIVE: BROOKLYN AT THE FOREFRONT

It was not uncommon in the postwar period for Brooklyn to be referred to as its own city. Although a half-century earlier, the formerly self-governing entity had joined with the four other boroughs to become part of New York City, Brooklyn's large size—nearly 2.9 million people in 1950[97]—and its enormous influence on postwar American culture made it seem like its own place. The *Saturday Evening Post* included an in-depth profile of Brooklyn in its series on American cities, and the literary travel magazine *Holiday* called the borough "a key city in the geography of the American mind" on its cover.[98] In 1947, Jackie Robinson had shattered baseball's color line at

97 If separated from New York City, Brooklyn would have been the third-largest city in the U.S. in 1950, trailing four-borough NYC (5 million) and Chicago (3.6 million) but well ahead of Philadelphia (2.1 million). The current estimate for Brooklyn is 2.6 million, which, if separated, would make it fourth behind NYC, Los Angeles, and Chicago.

98 William Fay, "The Cities of America: Brooklyn," *Saturday Evening Post* (3-25-1950) and Irwin Shaw, "Brooklyn," *Holiday* (June 1950).

Ebbets Field. Over the next few years, led by Arthur Miller, Norman Mailer and Marianne Moore, Brooklyn writers established a clear presence on the maps of the theater and literary worlds. From his tiny apartment on Mermaid Avenue in Coney Island, Woody Guthrie circulated lyrics of his seminal folk song "This Land Is Your Land." By the mid-1950s, Bensonhurst would serve as the fictional home of *The Honeymooners,* the popular working-class sitcom featuring comedian Jackie Gleason, who had grown up in Bed-Stuy. Meanwhile, Gleason's fellow comedians, including Greenpoint's legendary Mae West, Brownsville's Phil Silvers, and Bensonhurst's Howard brothers (aka the Three Stooges), brought Brooklyn's rich tradition of humor to Hollywood.[99]

Brooklyn may not have been its own city, but it nonetheless carved out its own identity. Unlike Manhattan, Brooklyn had grown horizontally rather than vertically. Completed in 1929, the thirty-seven-story Williamsburgh Bank Tower (informally known as the "clock tower") near the junction of Atlantic and Flatbush Avenues in downtown Brooklyn remained the borough's tallest edifice through the early twenty-first century. The stately

---

99 Among the other Hollywood stars from Brooklyn during the era were Barbara Stanwyck (Flatbush) and Susan Hayward (Prospect Heights). Hollywood racism prevented Lena Horne (Bed-Stuy) from gaining starring roles. Meanwhile, Mickey Rooney and Rita Hayworth were both born in Brooklyn but moved to Hollywood at a young age.

apartment buildings along Eastern Parkway topped out at six floors. Rather than its skyline, Brooklyn's built environment is best known for the three-story brownstones of Fort Greene, Bed-Stuy, and Park Slope. The low-rise architecture, in turn, contributed to the borough's identity as a place of residential quietude. Even so, the industrial area along the waterfront—from the docks of Red Hook through the Brooklyn Navy Yard to Greenpoint— remained quite dynamic. As documented by noted Brooklyn writer Irwin Shaw[100] in *Holiday*, "Brooklyn is industrially one of the five top cities in the country," with nearly seven thousand manufacturing plants, including one that Shaw reported to be "the largest coffee-roasting plant in the world."[101] When they returned home, those same people who worked on the waterfront and in the various factories could enjoy a bit more peace and quiet than their counterparts in Manhattan.

---

100   A product of the radical Group Theatre of the 1930s, Shaw (1913–1984) graduated from James Madison High School and became a leading novelist after publication of *The Young Ones* (1948), which a decade later became a popular Hollywood drama about World War II starring Marlon Brando and Montgomery Clift. Shaw's novel *Rich Man, Poor Man* (1970) became a TV mini-series in the mid-1970s that is notable for foregrounding class conflict. As he explains in the *Holiday* story, Shaw grew up in Sheepshead Bay and fondly recalled his summers spent at Coney Island.

101   Shaw presumably was referring to Albert Ehlers, Inc., which had recently purchased a 24,000-square-foot factory site in Bushwick. *New York Times* (4-7-1950). Earlier that year, the company's president (Albert Ehlers Jr.) noted that "Brooklyn is one of the principal coffee ports of the United States." *Brooklyn Eagle* (1-6-1950).

Mid-century Brooklyn was indeed a place where working-class people could attain middle-class comfort and stability, and the children of immigrants could afford to attend college. Social mobility also spawned anxiety, captured famously by Arthur Miller. And mid-century Brooklyn was by no means a utopia. As Shaw presented it, Brooklyn contained multiple contradictions. It was "devout," as evidenced by its 635 churches and 443 synagogues; but it was also "ungodly," with mobsters controlling the waterfront and lingering pro-Nazi sentiment in various quarters. It was "tolerant," as the Brooklyn Dodgers of 1947 onward embodied, but it was also "bigoted," as the redlined map of the borough created distinct patterns of residential segregation. It was "sophisticated," as illustrated by its successes in the world of arts and letters, but also "provincial," full of insular, xenophobic neighborhoods. As the journalist John Gunther observed in the best-selling political travelogue *Inside U.S.A.* (1947), Brooklyn was "a world in itself." Among its chief characteristics, Gunther said, were "a fierce local nationalism," the Dodgers, the waterfront docks, Coney Island, and "the *Tablet*, one of the most reactionary Catholic papers in the country."[102] During the first decade after the war, Brooklyn was nevertheless at the apex of its national influence.

102 Gunther, 554.

With the election of William O'Dwyer in the fall of 1945, Brooklyn had also regained City Hall after a two-decade hiatus. In his first term, O'Dwyer navigated difficult terrain. The strike wave that began before his election continued into the mayor's first year in office. In February 1946, a two-week tugboat strike shut down the waterfront, causing O'Dwyer to sound alarms regarding the city's supply of coal and oil in the middle of winter. As he would do frequently over the next decade, Mike Quill, the militant union leader of the transit workers, also threatened a subway strike. Under pressure from La Guardia and his crowd, O'Dwyer needed to prove that he wasn't restoring Tammany's rule. In early 1947, Gunther noted, the mayor thus "shook the organization up from top to bottom, removed some of its more adhesive members, and became, in effect, Tammany chieftain himself with the slate washed clean." The mayor had been a beat cop before becoming district attorney, and in Gunther's view, he was motivated by both "[t]he urge to get ahead" and "to do something for the little fellow."[103]

With Robert Moses calling the shots, the mayor embarked on many of the plans that the builder had mapped out with La Guardia. Throughout his first year in office, O'Dwyer and Moses also pushed for New York City to become the permanent home of the United Nations. At the time the city was competing against San Francisco, Boston, and Philadelphia. As Robert Caro explained in *The Power Broker*, it was Moses who made it happen in New York by recruiting John D. Rockefeller Jr. to purchase, then donate the property that became the UN's current home on the East River. Work began on the project in the summer of 1947. O'Dwyer would later say that he believed the project was "the one great thing that would make the city the center of the world."[104] The mayor's efforts earned him the lasting support of Eleanor Roosevelt, who remained a driving force behind the UN's work through the 1950s. O'Dwyer's embrace of the organization also gained him noisy enemies from his home borough. Presiding over the Brooklyn diocese in Prospect Heights, far-right priest Father Edward Curran denounced the UN as "a foreign sovereignty."[105]

In October 1947 the UN held hearings on Palestine at its temporary home at Lake Success in Great Neck (on Long Island). One of the leading Zionist figures who testified on behalf of the initial "Partition Plan" for Palestine was Rabbi Abba Hillel Silver. Somewhat surprisingly, Silver was from neither Manhattan nor Brooklyn, but from Cleveland. The

---

104   Caro, 771–775.

105   As reported in the *New York Times* (10-4-1947), Curran tried to stop the city from transferring the deed to the UN site in court.

city's foremost advocate for the creation of Israel was thus Eleanor Roosevelt. Since its inception in 1945, Eleanor had served on the UN's Social, Humanitarian and Cultural Committee, which oversaw world health, the plight of refugees, human rights, and issues of women's equality. In that capacity Roosevelt paid particular attention to the aftermath of the Holocaust. "I would like to see Palestine opened to the homeless Jews of the world," Roosevelt told the *New York Times* in late 1946.[106] Amid the fall 1947 meeting at Lake Success, the Truman administration—prodded by Rabbi Silver's outreach to Republican leaders ahead of the following year's election—announced its support for Partition. FDR's point man on Holocaust refugee relief, Henry Morgenthau, declared that "the Jews of America owe a debt of gratitude" to President Truman, Secretary of State George Marshall and Eleanor Roosevelt.[107] Despite opposition from Egypt, Saudi Arabia, Iran, Iraq, India, and eight other member-states, the UN General Assembly endorsed the plan at the end of November 1947.

Six months later, after the Israeli Declaration of Independence on May 14 and an attempt to reclaim

---

106 S.J. Woolf, "The New Chapter in Mrs. Roosevelt's Life," *New York Times* (12-15-1946). As the reporter noted, Eleanor believed the UN was "important for women because it means they will have a hand in building the peace." The story also reported that Eleanor was considered the "hardest-working delegate" at the UN, spending six days per week from 9 a.m.–7:30 p.m.

107 *New York Times* (10-13-1947).

Palestine by a coalition of Arab states the following day, the liberal *New York Post* closely tracked a conflict of obvious interest to the paper's many Jewish readers.[108] A few days after the conflict broke out, the paper reported that a capacity crowd at Madison Square Garden for a "Salute to Israel" rally—featuring speeches by Mayor O'Dwyer and Rabbi Silver—had caused 75,000 people to be turned away. The *Post*'s James Weschler explained that Henry Wallace, who had announced his run as a third-party candidate for president in the fall election, addressed a stadium in Los Angeles filled with 30,000 supporters (including marquee figures Charlie Chaplin, Edward G. Robinson, and Dalton Trumbo).[109] Warning that the conflict over the former Palestine could be "another Spain," the Cold War dove Wallace urged the U.S. to back Israel. Ted Thackeray, husband of *Post* owner Dorothy Schiff and the paper's co-publisher, argued in a lengthy editorial that the actions of the Arab states violated the UN Security Council's charter. As a result, Thackeray declared, it was now the Council's "obligation to stop the war of invasion and conquest on which the Arab world has embarked." Such an action, he averred, not

---

108   Earlier that year, the *Post* had merged with the *Bronx Home News*, giving it a strong presence in the Jewish sections of three boroughs, including the Sanders family's Midwood area.

109   Located on Beverley Boulevard in Fairfax, the Gilmore Stadium site is now the home of CBS Television City and next door to the Los Angeles Museum of the Holocaust.

only amounted to a defense of Israel but was "a defense of law." Echoing Wallace at a separate Madison Square Garden rally, left-wing Congressman Vito Marcantonio, head of the American Labor Party and a longtime La Guardia ally, called for the U.S. to support Israel, viewing the battle as a continuation of the fight against fascism. In Brooklyn, ALP-backed Democrat Emanuel Celler, a leading Israel supporter who represented greater East Flatbush (adjacent to the Sanders family's district) won reelection in 1948 with over 80 percent of the vote. Indeed, there were few voices of objection in New York City to the placement of the new nation. That David Ben-Gurion, Israel's first prime minister, had come out of the socialist tradition of Labor Zionism further solidified left support. For the Sanders family and their millions of peers who had been devastated by the Holocaust, Israel stood as a welcome refuge.[110]

Eleanor Roosevelt remained a familiar presence in Brooklyn well into the following decade. In addition to her daily column (which appeared in the mostly conservative *World-Telegram*, and by the late 1950s in the *Post*), Eleanor could be heard regularly on the radio. From the fall of 1948 through the end of 1949, she and her daughter Anna were carried by the ABC Radio network. Next, from early 1950

110   *New York Post* (5-15-1948 through 5-18-1948). First elected in 1922, Celler would hold his seat until his defeat by Elizabeth Holtzman in 1972. Like Bernie Sanders, Holtzman was born in 1941. She graduated from Abraham Lincoln High School in Coney Island.

through the following summer, Eleanor held forth about
her UN work on a show heard daily on NBC radio. Eleanor's
visits to Brooklyn also garnered media attention. In addition to partnering with leading organizations like the
Jewish Philanthropic League of Brooklyn, Roosevelt and her
inner circle worked closely with the borough's chapter of
the NAACP. When black leaders protested a spate of NYPD
violence in the spring of 1949, Eleanor's ally Mayor O'Dwyer
named FDR Jr. to head up an investigatory committee.[111] A
few months later, Eleanor addressed an NAACP gathering at
the Concord Baptist Church in Bed-Stuy, where Brooklyn's
leading black minister Gardner Taylor presided. After being
introduced by NAACP's Roy Wilkins, Roosevelt declared
that "It is essential that we make the United States a real
democracy where all citizens have equal rights." The former
First Lady turned UN figurehead also told a gathering at the
Brooklyn Jewish Center in Crown Heights that the found-
ing of Israel mirrored that of the United States. She visited
Midwood High School (located next to Brooklyn College) in
order to receive an award. And at one point the Edward H.
Levine Association, a political club based on Ocean Avenue
in Midwood, tried unsuccessfully to draft the former First
Lady to run for governor against Tom Dewey.[112]

---

111   *New York Times* (4-29-1949).

112   *Brooklyn Eagle* (6-15-1949, 1-31-1952, 4-28-1952 and 7-31-1950).

Like most of her followers, Eleanor was pro-United Nations, anti-Communist, and a stalwart Democrat. That combination led her to endorse Truman in 1948, who faced challengers including New York's Dewey and Henry Wallace, FDR's former vice president. The Cold War was the central issue in the campaign, with Truman more often attacking the Republican Party's strong isolationist wing rather than Dewey, a moderate who supported interventionism. The Democrats also had solid support from organized labor because of the Republicans' postwar assault on unions. On the Friday night before Election Day, Truman traveled through Brooklyn in a festive motorcade tour that led him from Williamsburg through Bed-Stuy to the Brooklyn Academy of Music in Fort Greene. According to the *Brooklyn Eagle*, along Bedford Avenue the "streets were jammed with people" including "women in house dresses, shopkeepers in their aprons, and laborers still in their working clothes." Bands entertained large gatherings near the Bed-Stuy YMCA and on Fulton Street. Outside of BAM, 1,800 police officers kept the massive crowd under control. Inside, a full house of 3,500 people heard Truman denounce the Republicans for trying to kill the Marshall Plan and attack Wallace because of his support from Communists.[113]

113   *Brooklyn Eagle* (10-30-1948).

Eleanor's support helped Truman prevail narrowly over Dewey in 1948, with Wallace finishing a distant fourth, behind segregationist Strom Thurmond. Because of his resume and the fact that he had many high-profile supporters (including Brooklynites Norman Mailer, Arthur Miller, and Woody Guthrie), Wallace had initially been viewed as a formidable contender. As Cold War tensions escalated, the candidate's ties to the American Labor Party and the CPUSA subjected Wallace to Red-baiting. Though not a Communist, the former vice-president nonetheless was calling for dialogue with the Soviet Union in opposition to the hardliner Truman. In New York State, he was running on the ballot line of the American Labor Party, which remained an active electoral presence in the first few elections after the war. In 1946, the ALP had joined with Republicans in nearly unseating a Democratic congressman on the Brooklyn waterfront; meanwhile, Vito Marcantonio won reelection running on both the ALP and Democratic lines. Although he got crushed in November 1948, [114] Wallace took solace in the fact that his ally Marcantonio had won reelection in East Harlem,

114   Nationally, Wallace ran as the candidate of the short-lived Progressive Party; in New York State, he was on the ALP ballot line. Despite his poor national showing (2.5 percent), Wallace pulled in nearly 425,000 votes in New York City (13 percent), with over 165,000 coming from Brooklyn. In the Sanders family's district, Wallace tallied over 14,000—only 2,500 less than Dewey but well short of Truman's nearly 41,500. For results, see *New York Times* (11-3-1948).

this time only on the ALP line; in addition to a Democratic challenger, Marcantonio defeated a Republican backed by the ALP's splinter group the Liberal Party. In terms of electoral politics, New York City's radical left was still a significant force.

Marcantonio sought to expand that influence by challenging Mayor O'Dwyer's bid for reelection in 1949. "Marc" called out the incumbent for appeasing large real estate interests and for raising the subway fare from a nickel to a dime, and he made civil rights and housing segregation his central issues. Marc was closely allied with black leaders from Harlem as well as Puerto Rican activists from what was becoming known as Spanish Harlem. But he also waged a spirited citywide campaign that brought him to Brighton Beach, Brownsville, and Red Hook on the day before the election.[115] Good-government candidate Newbold Morris, who La Guardia had supported four years earlier, challenged O'Dwyer on the Republican and Liberal Party lines. Backed by Governor Dewey and Fiorello's widow Marie La Guardia (who campaigned for him in Brooklyn),[116] Morris invoked the Little Flower in

---

115 For details of the campaign, see Meyer, 39; and Martha Biondi, *To Stand and Fight: The Struggle for Civil Rights in Postwar New York City* (Cambridge, MA: Harvard University Press, 2006), 209–211.

116 On the Saturday before the election, Marie attended a campaign tea event for Morris at the Hotel Granada near the Brooklyn Academy of Music. *Brooklyn Eagle* (11-6-1949).

denouncing O'Dwyer's ties to Tammany. The two challengers split the anti-machine vote, enabling O'Dwyer to win easily. Meanwhile, the ALP's candidate for Brooklyn borough president, Ada Jackson—a black organizer from Bed-Stuy with Communist ties[117]—took in 12 percent of the vote. While no longer influential on Election Day, the ALP would continue to organize around civil rights and tenant issues over the next few years.

Soon after his reelection, O'Dwyer faced a firestorm of controversy initiated by a most-unexpected source: the *Brooklyn Eagle,* the same Democratic machine outlet that had strongly supported his three runs for mayor. "Lucrative Borough Rackets Feed Vast Crime Syndicate" announced the headline of part one of the *Eagle*'s weeklong series on Sunday, December 11, 1949. Investigative reporter Ed Reid continued to serve up a steady dose of explosive charges over the next five days, after which the *Eagle* milked the story with headlines trumpeting the outcry from prosecutors, elected officials, and clergy. According to Reid, a Bay Ridge-based gambling ring had ensnared Brooklynites from the borough's docks to its schools, including the elementary grades. "Gamblers Infest Schools, Prey on Kids' Lunch Money," read one shocking

---

117   On its front page two days after the election (11-10-1946), the *Eagle* reported that Jackson flew to Moscow one day earlier in order to represent the CPUSA-affiliated Congress of American Women at a meeting of the Women's International Democratic Federation.

headline. The story was accompanied by photos of sample betting cards given to youngsters with slates of college and pro football and college hoops to choose from. According to the hard-boiled Reid, "The syndicate's bookies infest the schools of Brooklyn and the rest of the city like rats infest a granary." The muckraker had been working with O'Dwyer's successor as Brooklyn DA, Miles McDonald, to expose the nefarious activity. Although the mayor was not immediately implicated by the revelations, O'Dwyer was forced to reckon with the fact that his police force was directly involved. And it wasn't just a few rogue cops. As the *Eagle* reported in a story placed above the paper's front-page logo, between "eight and nine thousand" NYPD officers "in Brooklyn alone" were allegedly implicated in providing protection for the borough's bookies. It was a stunning expose, based on alarmist accounts and inflated numbers. But the follow-up investigations remained in the headlines across the city over the next nine months until President Truman suddenly appointed O'Dwyer as US ambassador to Mexico in August 1950. After devouring one of its own, Brooklyn would not regain City Hall until the perilous 1970s.[118]

118   See *Brooklyn Eagle* (12-11-1949 through 12-18-1949). In the wake of Truman's announcement, an *Eagle* editorial (8-16-1950) shed light on why O'Dwyer went down. Prior to announcing that he would run again in 1949, O'Dwyer had given serious consideration to not doing so (for health reasons). One of the people he approached to run in his place was Brooklyn borough president John Cashmore, who doubled as the

City Council President Vincent Impellitteri, a Manhattan Democrat, became interim mayor, with another election slated for November 1950. Convinced that the acting mayor would not win, Tammany chose Ferdinand Pecora. Then a judge, Tammany's pick had gained fame early in the New Deal by presiding over the Pecora Commission, which exposed the Wall Street fraud that helped cause the Great Depression. (The commission, in turn, led to the passage of the Glass-Steagall Act in 1934, separating investment houses from commercial banks.) A strident anti-Communist, Pecora ran on the Democratic and Liberal Party lines. Skeptical of Impellitteri because of his longstanding ties to Tammany prior to 1950, the Republicans chose Edward Corsi, a La Guardia ally. Undeterred, the acting mayor formed the Experience Party and ran on its line. Corsi attacked both of his opponents' Tammany links and highlighted Pecora's connections to Frank Costello, the leading mafia figurehead based in Manhattan. The pivotal moment in the election came when it was revealed that Democratic and Liberal Party leaders had offered to make Impellitteri a judge if he dropped out of the race. That allowed the acting mayor—who stressed

borough's Democratic boss. The withdrawn offer resulted in bad blood between the two, and Cashmore then pressured DA McDonald to go after the mayor. McDonald never proved that O'Dwyer was involved in the scandal. But since it happened under his watch, O'Dwyer took the fall. Reid and the *Brooklyn Eagle*, meanwhile, won a 1951 Pulitzer Prize for reporting the story throughout 1950.

that he remained a Democrat—to present himself as the anti-Tammany candidate. Notably, no candidate sought O'Dwyer's blessing. Propelled by a whopping margin from Queens, Impellitteri prevailed over Pecora by more than 200,000 votes. For the first three years of the second half of the twentieth century, the nation's most important city was led by a third-party candidate.[119]

119 For issues in the race, see *New York Times* (10-24-1950 and 11-8-1950). All three main candidates were from Manhattan. In Brooklyn, Pecora defeated the acting mayor by less than 10,000 votes (but prevailed over Impellitteri in the Sanders family's district by 13,000). Corsi barely reached 15 percent citywide and in Midwood district only defeated the fourth-place challenger, the ALP's Paul Ross, by 1,500 votes. Ross, a civil rights activist, polled 150,000 citywide, one-third from Brooklyn. The ALP's candidate for Senate that year was none other than W.E.B. DuBois, who tallied over 50,000 votes in Brooklyn (while losing overwhelmingly to Democratic stalwart Herbert Lehman). Results in *Brooklyn Eagle* (11-8-1950).

CHAPTER SIX:
THE EBONY EXPRESS

As its explosive gambling series wound down in late 1949, the *Brooklyn Eagle* featured a front-page photo of Jackie Robinson. With Christmas approaching, the Dodgers star and national icon of integration was shown handing autographed baseball equipment to two homeless toddlers, one white and one black. As the caption explained, Robinson also "issued a call for persons interested in adopting or boarding youngsters to write to him care of the Dodgers." The photo's placement and text illustrated the degree to which Robinson had become a household name, both in Brooklyn and across the nation. It also captured Robinson's commitment to social issues outside the baseball diamond. Most notable of all, perhaps, was the personal dimension, with Robinson soliciting help and explaining where to reach him. Brooklyn at mid-century may have been a de facto city of nearly three million people, but it still presented itself as an intimate place.

The 1949 season had been Robinson's best since he broke the color line two years earlier. He was the National League (NL) batting champion (.342), led the majors in stolen bases (37) and came in second in the NL in runs batted in (124). The Dodgers reached the World Series, losing to their rivals from the Bronx in five games. Jackie's regular-season's performance earned him NL Most Valuable Player honors, putting the third-year player in the elite company of recent winners including Stan Musial and the American League's Ted Williams and Joe DiMaggio. But Robinson's exceptional performance on the field wasn't what generated the most headlines that summer. Instead, it was his mid-July testimony before the House Un-American Activities Committee (HUAC) that came amidst Cold War anti-Communist hysteria. As shown by Robinson's foremost biographer Arnold Rampersad, the NAACP had tried to stop Jackie from testifying because of the group's concerns about HUAC's crackdown on dissent.[120] But Robinson was prodded by Dodgers president Branch Rickey, who had broken the de facto ban on black players when he signed Robinson in 1945. An anti-Communist Republican with ties to Governor Dewey, Rickey was also a member of Brooklyn's Plymouth Church, the historic abolitionist

---

120   Arnold Rampersad, *Jackie Robinson: A Biography* (New York: Knopf, 1997), 210–211.

stronghold.[121] On Monday, July 18, 1949, Jackie and his wife Rachel Robinson flew down to DC.

Robinson had been summoned by HUAC in order to provide what the committee hoped would be damning views of Paul Robeson, the popular left-wing black actor and singer. Throughout the preceding fifteen years Robeson had worked closely with Communists but never officially joined the party. HUAC chair John S. Wood, a Georgia Democrat, wanted Robinson, the great symbol of American integration, to attack Robeson for a controversial comment the activist had made that spring. At a leftist gathering in Paris, Robeson declared that it was "unthinkable" that blacks would fight in a war against the Soviet Union because of that nation's commitment to racial equality.[122] Jackie had served in the segregated U.S. Army during World War II, overcoming racist hostility while stationed at Fort Hood, Texas. He then broke baseball's color line at Ebbets Field in April of 1947, and fifteen months later, President Truman issued an executive order

---

121 Rickey's ties to Dewey are mentioned in *Branch Rickey*, a 2011 bio by the legendary New York City journalist Jimmy Breslin. The Plymouth Church website mentions that Rickey was a member: http://www.plymouthchurch. org/history. For further details regarding the church's abolitionist history, see Theodore Hamm, ed. *Frederick Douglass in Brooklyn* (Brooklyn, NY: Akashic Books, 2017).

122 As Rampersad observes (p.212), Robeson's statement was open to dual interpretations—i.e., it was either a call for "mass treason" or a comment regarding the lack of racial equality in the U.S. Given the Cold War climate, the former "carried the day" in the press.

integrating the U.S. armed forces. The national spotlight was thus on Robinson when he went before HUAC, which relaxed its rules on press photographs in order to enhance the spectacle.

The irony of the fact that he had been asked to attack Robeson was not lost on Robinson. A former star athlete at Rutgers, Robeson stood at the forefront of the campaign to integrate baseball. Amid his celebrated Broadway run as Othello in December 1943, the actor tried to win over Major League Baseball's segregationist commissioner Kenesaw Mountain Landis, who had tried to deflect growing criticism from the black press by insisting there was no written rule establishing a color line in the game. Prior to remarks given by leading black publishers including those from the *Amsterdam News, Pittsburgh Courier,* and *Baltimore Afro-American,* Robeson addressed the gathering of Landis and team executives. According to Rampersad, the performer "argued so powerfully for an end to Jim Crow in baseball that the owners gave him a 'rousing ovation,'" even as they refused to act on the issue.[123] In his lengthy recap of the meeting, versatile left-wing *Amsterdam News* columnist Dan Burley named Robinson and his future Dodgers star teammate Roy Campanella as two standout

123   Ibid.

Negro Leagues players that could break the color barrier.[124]
Meanwhile, the New York City-based Communist Party
had been spearheading the campaign for the integration
of America's national pastime since 1936. Lester Rodney,
the *Daily Worker*'s Bensonhurst-raised sports reporter,
provided a steady stream of coverage of the issue through
the war years, even as most of the local mainstream press
ignored it. After Jackie signed with the Dodgers, he and
Rodney became friendly. When Robinson made his debut
at Ebbets in 1947, Rodney told *Daily Worker* readers that
the "depths of cheers for Robinson [reflected] real democracy . . . Cheer on for a while, you people of Brooklyn! Cheer
on, democracy!"[125]

What Robinson told HUAC regarding his views of
Robeson was fairly tame. As the cameras flashed, Jackie
explained that his "sense of responsibility" had motivated
him to speak to the committee. "Every single Negro who
is worth his salt is going to resent any kinds of slurs and

---

124   *New York Amsterdam News* (12-11-1943). Burley was a noted jazz
      musician, friend of Langston Hughes, and lexicographer of the era's
      black slang. As he stressed in his column regarding the Landis meeting,
      "Jim Crow in baseball is as unfair, odious, and un-American as Jim Crow"
      on buses and trains or in the armed forces, restaurants, hotels, etc. He
      also called out owners of Negro League teams for not opposing it.

125   *Daily Worker* (4-15-1947). Rampersad (p. 120) mentions Rodney as an
      early Robinson ally. As Rodney (1911–2009) later recalled, "For me and
      the other kids on my block in Bensonhurst, Ebbets Field was a magical
      place." Angelo Trento and Irwin Silber, *Press Box Red: The Story of Press
      Box Red: The Communist Who Helped Break the Color Line in Sports*
      (Philadelphia: Temple University Press, 2003), 22.

discrimination because of his race," he declared. Yet, just because it's "a Communist who denounces injustice in the courts, police brutality and lynching," Robinson said, that "doesn't change the truth of their charges." Jim Crow, Jackie noted, had predated the advent of the Communist Party in the U.S. At this point, the celebrated ballplayer appeared to be making a resounding statement on behalf of freedom of speech. But when he turned his focus to Robeson, Robinson provided the headlines. He first showed respect, calling Robeson "a great singer and actor." Yet in Jackie's view, while Robeson "had a right to [express] his personal views," the entertainer's statements about the unwillingness of blacks to fight versus the Soviet Union were "very silly." "They'd [black people] do their best to help the country win the war—against Russia or any other enemy that threatened us," he assured the committee. Blacks, Robinson averred, believed their future lay in America and would not be tempted by a "siren song sung in bass," a slam against what he viewed as Robeson's delivery of Communist propaganda set to music. After the HUAC session ended, Jackie and Rachel flew home in time for the Dodgers home game under the lights at Ebbets. The "Ebony Express," as the *Eagle* called Jackie, was in MVP form, complete with one of his signature steals of home in a 3–0 victory over the Cubs.[126]

126   See Rampersad, 213–215; and *Amsterdam News* (7-23-1949).

That week saw a flurry of positive news coverage regarding Robinson's testimony. Under the headline "Credo of an American," the liberal *New York Post* excerpted Jackie's remarks in an editorial. For the conservative *Daily News*, Robinson was "quite a man," "quite a ballplayer," and "quite a credit to his race" (a common condescending phrase of the era).[127] That week's *Amsterdam News* printed Robeson's response on its front page. "The whole thing was an insult to the Negro people," he declared, adding, "There's no argument between Jackie and me." The activist entertainer then cited the fact that insurance companies including Stuyvesant Town developer Met Life owned most of the farms in the South; and that HUAC members, including its chair, had voiced no outrage at recent lynchings of black World War II veterans in Georgia. That same edition of the city's leading black paper also reported that it had surveyed 239 Brooklyn residents, white and black. Not one disagreed with Jackie's critique of Robeson. The Dodgers' "sensational second baseman," said the *Amsterdam News*, "was batting 1.000" in Brooklyn.[128]

After the dust settled for a few weeks, it was Jackie who kicked it up again, this time with an assist from the *Brooklyn*

---

127 Rampersad, 215.

128 *Amsterdam News* (7-23-1949). Alas, after tracking the baseball integration closely through Robinson's debut and beyond, Dan Burley stopped writing for the publication in 1948.

Eagle's lead reporter Ed Reid. Beginning Monday, August 15, the paper ran a ten-part front-page series in which Jackie told his life story to Reid. The bulk of the installments did not contain explosive material, as Robinson particularly focused on the hostilities he faced during his high school years in Pasadena, California, and his experience in the army. But on the final day of the series, Jackie's discussion of his HUAC testimony one month earlier set off fireworks. "Robeson Has the 'Wrong Outlook'—Robinson," read the headline of the story that ran above the *Eagle*'s logo. Although Jackie noted that "I don't think I can speak for the 15,000,000 Negroes in the country—but neither can Paul Robeson," freedom of speech was no longer the ballplayer's primary concern. Robinson declared that his view represented the sentiments of an overwhelming majority of Americans. He told Reid that he received "boxes of letters regarding my testimony in Washington" and that "99 percent" of the missives were "friendly." "In Russia," the ballplayer added, "I don't think they would get through the mails."[129] The statements were reprinted across the nation, and Robeson was now public enemy number one. On the very next day—Saturday, August 27, 1949—an angry mob of Cold War zealots attacked a crowd consisting largely of black and Jewish Communists attending a

---

129   Series in *Brooklyn Eagle* (8-15-1949 through 8-19-1949; and 8-22-1949 through 8-26-1949). Robeson comments on 8-26-1949.

Robeson concert in Peekskill, New York, less than sixty miles from Brooklyn. Upset about the mob's actions at the time, Robinson later expressed regret for helping lead the crusade against Robeson.[130]

By the fall of 1949, Jackie was Brooklyn's most prominent national figure—yet he and his family no longer called the borough home. When he and Rachel first arrived in the spring of 1947, they spent their first two weeks in Manhattan at the Hotel McAlpin on Herald Square. While there, an enterprising Brooklynite named Mabel Brown showed up unannounced and proposed that the couple and their baby (Jackie Jr., born in 1946) share her apartment in the increasingly black neighborhood of Bed-Stuy. The Robinsons accepted the offer but when they arrived at 526 MacDonough Street, they found out it was a cramped, roach-infested tenement. Black friends of the Robinsons then bought a duplex at 5224 Tilden Avenue in East Flatbush, a Jewish neighborhood. The protestations of many white neighbors notwithstanding, Jackie and his family rented the top floor—and became life-long friends with the Salows, a Russian-American family who lived two doors down.[131] By the summer of 1949, as the Dodgers star proudly told Reid, the couple had moved to Queens, where they had

130   Rampersad, 216.

131   Ibid., p. 180; and Jonathan Eig, *Opening Day: The Story of Jackie Robinson's First Season* (New York: Simon & Schuster, 2007), 148–159.

"a bigger backyard for Jackie Jr." and white next-door neighbors with whom they "g[o]t along fine."[132] Following Dodger teammate Roy Campanella's lead, the Robinsons bought a two-story, $30,000 Tudor Revival house located at 112-40 177th Street in St. Albans. After a whites-only covenant had been broken earlier in the decade, a slew of successful black figures had moved to the neighborhood. *Ebony* reported that the Robinsons' neighbors included jazz legends Illinois Jacquet and Cootie Williams.[133] Brooklyn's own Lena Horne, along with the great bandleader Count Basie and preeminent black intellectual W.E.B. DuBois, also called St. Albans home at the time. Even though he lived in Queens (and later Connecticut) in the 1950s, Jackie would remain active in Brooklyn throughout the rest of his career on and off the field.

Like countless numbers of kids growing up in Brooklyn, Larry and Bernie Sanders were avid fans of their "hometown" team. "We went to Ebbets Field as often as we could," says Larry. "We loved the Dodgers!" As the *Guardian* reported in 2015, Bernie can still rattle off the names of the starting infield from the teams of the early 1950s.[134] While at first glance that may sound no different

132   *Brooklyn Eagle* (8-25-1949 and 8-26-1949).

133   *Ebony* (Vol. 6, 1950).

134   Les Carpenter, "How the Dodgers and Baseball Shaped Bernie Sanders' World View, *The Guardian* (10-27-2015).

than politicians from other major-league cities, it is important to keep in mind that the Dodgers' pluralism extended well beyond just Jackie Robinson. The team's stars included black pitcher Don Newcombe and Roy Campanella, the son of an Italian-American father and African-American mother; distinctly ethnic whites including Pee Wee Reese (a Southerner who befriended Robinson) and Carl Furillo; and white sluggers Gil Hodges and Duke Snider. After losing the World Series four times to the Yankees since Robinson joined the team, the Dodgers finally triumphed over their cross-town rivals in 1955. When Newcombe took the mound that season, Brooklyn's starting lineup often consisted of a black majority, with Jackie at third base, Junior Gilliam at second, Cuban-born Sandy Amoros in left, and Campanella behind the plate. Making his rookie debut that year was Sandy Koufax, the Brooklyn-raised southpaw who became a star after the team moved to Los Angeles and remains one of the great Jewish athletes of all time.[135] While the Willie Mays-led New York Giants fielded a similar number of black players at the time at the Polo Grounds in Harlem, the Yankees lineup in 1955 featured only one, outfielder (and later catcher) Elston Howard,

---

135   Raised in Borough Park and Bensonhurst, Koufax (b. 1935) attended Lafayette High School in Bath Beach (near Bensonhurst). Other distinguished Lafayette graduates include legendary children's book illustrator Maurice Sendak (1928–2012), creator of *Where the Wild Things Are*; and longtime CNN talk-show host Larry King (b. 1933).

who had just broken the team's color line that year. The nostalgia that the Sanders brothers and their peers share for the Brooklyn Dodgers of the 1950s is thus suffused with multicultural idealism.

CHAPTER SEVEN:
THE SALESMAN

"The effect of the play on people is a little frightening."

—Arthur Miller, regarding *Death of a Salesman* (1949)

Playwright Arthur Miller, who attended high school in Coney Island, was a resident of Brooklyn Heights throughout the 1940s. After initial success as a nonfiction writer, Miller had gained fame in the theater world amid the successful Broadway run of his play *All My Sons*, which premiered in 1947 and won the New York Drama Critics Circle award (famously beating out Eugene O'Neill's classic work *The Iceman Cometh*). *Sons* is set in World War II, and its main character is a war profiteer who sold defective equipment that caused the deaths of twenty-one pilots. The family-centered drama dealt with many of the same themes regarding America's materialist values as *Death of a Salesman*. Miller dedicated *Sons* to Elia Kazan, the noted director who would also bring *Salesman* to the stage. Along with Bronx-raised Lee J. Cobb (the actor playing *Salesman*'s lead character Willy Loman), Kazan was a product of New York City's left-wing Group Theatre of the 1930s. Clifford Odets and Marc Blitzstein were the Group's most prominent playwrights, and John Garfield, Stella Adler, Canada Lee, and Cobb were its foremost actors. The Group was a leading participant in the CPUSA's "Popular Front" movement, which enlisted the arts in the fight against the rising tide of fascism in Europe. Because they traveled in the CPUSA's orbit, many of the Group's leading figures—including Odets, Garfield, Kazan, and Cobb (as well as Miller, because he worked closely with Kazan and other members)—were subject to scrutiny by the House Un-American Activities Committee during the Second Red Scare and McCarthy era.[136]

On the day before *Salesman* opened in mid-February 1949, readers of the *New York Post* perhaps took note of the latest column by the paper's influential theater critic Vernon Rice. Under the headline "Arthur Miller Amazed by Pre-Broadway Success," Rice explained that in order to create buzz around the Broadway premiere, producers Kermit Bloomgarden (who grew up in Williamsburg, Brooklyn) and Walter Fried had opened the play three

---

136 For more details on the innumerable left-wing cultural creators and movements that aligned with the Popular Front during the mid-1930s through World War II, as well as their legacy in the postwar period, see Michael Denning's encyclopedic 1996 work *The Cultural Front: The Laboring of American Culture in the Twentieth Century* (Verso).

weeks earlier in Philadelphia. The duo sent special invitations to 150 local theater devotees for a Friday night dress rehearsal. Word of mouth spread quickly, and by the middle of the next week, the entire two-week run at the 1,600-seat Locust Theatre in Philly's Center City had sold out. "Nobody could be prepared for such a terrific reception," Miller explained, as he and Rice sat together in the office of James Proctor, the playwright's publicist and close friend. "You don't even dream such big things will happen," Miller said, noting that "you would have to be a very vain man if you did." As Rice detailed, the Philly marketing ploy spurred huge advance sales for the Broadway run, breaking the usual pattern in which theatergoers first waited to read the reviews before purchasing tickets. Instead, eager Broadway patrons had lined up on a rainy Monday morning during *Salesman*'s opening week outside the box office of the Morosco Theatre on West 45th Street. The show's run at the Morosco spanned the next four years.[137]

As the curtain was about to go up on Broadway, Miller explained his understanding of the play and the impact he had seen on its Philly audiences. "It's the story of a man who has a fatally enlarged image of himself and of what society requires of him in order to be a success," he told Rice.

---

137   *New York Post* (2-9-1949). Bloomgarden would later produce successful Broadway shows including *The Diary of Anne Frank* (1955) and *The Music Man* (1957).

Willy Loman famously grapples with the meaning of the American Dream as he struggles to stay afloat financially while also fretting about the values that he has imparted to his two grown sons. Biff, the elder son, is a former high school football star who now seeks a rustic life out west; meanwhile, his younger brother, "Happy," is caught up in the New York City rat race, trying to get rich. After getting fired, Willy ends up killing himself in order to provide life insurance money for his family. "The effect of the play on people is a little frightening," Miller said, adding that patrons "become proselytes. A reality, a mighty phenomenon, seems to be happening." Miller did not clarify exactly what that phenomenon was. But given the play's tragic resolution, the only plausible meaning is that Miller's work had shaken his audiences' faith in capitalist values. The playwright was careful not to be blunt about that message, however. "I'm not trying to sell anything," Miller told Rice. "I've just tried to make a totally honest portrait of my characters." His archetypal salesman was indeed a mid-twentieth-century common man. According to Miller, "We are all Willy Lomans, I guess—and are bothered by the same things."[138]

---

138   Ibid. In "Tragedy and the Common Man," an essay he wrote for the *New York Times* a few weeks after the play opened, Miller offered a democratic conception of tragedy. No longer the domain of Shakespeare's kings, tragedy in his view conveyed "the heart and spirit of the average man." *New York Times* (2-27-1949).

Like Miller, Loman called Brooklyn home, a fact high-lighted in local press coverage of the play. At the outset of Act One, it's clear that *Salesman* is set in the New York City area. When told by his wife, Linda, that "you look terrible," Willy explains that his frazzled nerves gave him problems behind the wheel of his car, causing his trip home from Yonkers to take four hours. The specific location is soon established. As the *Brooklyn Eagle* observed, Loman's "home was in Brooklyn but across the street a new apartment house had shut out the sun his garden would need. This was beginning of his despair." This familiar Brooklyn experience could have happened in any number of neighborhoods, including the Sanders family's Midwood terrain. As noted in a *New York Times* preview, the stage set—created by leading Broadway designer Jo Mielziner—was "a model of countless such homes in Brooklyn where Miller grew up after moving to Flatbush [actually Midwood] from Harlem as a boy." But on the two occasions in the play when Brooklyn is directly named, there's no reference to a particular neighborhood. The only precise marker comes early in Act One, when Biff and Happy reminisce about a girl named Betsy, who lived "over on Bushwick Avenue." This placed the Lomans somewhere in the greater Bushwick area, where new apartment buildings did indeed cast shadows over the area's many single-family houses. Regardless of the home's exact address,

Willy Loman's yearnings for bucolic quietude corre-
sponded with mid-century Brooklyn's identity as a place
that offered suburban tranquility in a bustling city.[139]

The play's immediate Broadway success made Miller
a star beyond just the theater world—and that celebrity
status conflicted with the playwright's cultivated working-class identity. In "Arthur Miller Grew in Brooklyn,"
the *Times*' Murray Schumach, a Brownsville native, profiled the playwright on the Sunday prior to *Salesman*'s
Thursday night premiere. As Schumach explained, before
his writing career Miller (then in his early thirties) had
worked as a truck driver, waiter, and crewman on a tanker.
Despite now making his living with his typewriter, Miller
told Schumach that he spent a few weeks working in a
factory each year. "Anyone who doesn't know what it's
like to stand in place for eight hours a day," Miller opined,
"doesn't know what it's all about. It's the only way you
can understand what makes men go into a gin mill after
work and start fighting."[140] Distinguishing himself from
his contemporaries, Miller added that "you don't learn

---

139   *Brooklyn Eagle* (2-11-1949) and *New York Times* (2-6-1949). Also see
      Theodore Hamm, "Arthur Miller's Brooklyn Legacy," *Brooklyn Rail* (March
      2005). There was no actual Willy Loman listed in the 1949 Brooklyn
      Telephone Directory. There was a Hal Loman living on Eastern Parkway
      in Brownsville, however.

140   *New York Times* (2-6-1949). Schumach spent nearly four more decades
      at the *Times*, establishing his reputation as a tireless general assignment
      reporter. See *New York Times* (11-28-2004).

about those things at Sardi's," referring to Broadway's late-night gathering place. Things changed after *Salesman* opened, with Miller becoming a household name. Brooks Atkinson, the era's leading theater critic, showered praise on the production in the *Times*. "By common consent," Atkinson insisted, "this is one of the finest dramas in the whole range of American theatre."[141] As Henry Luce's *Time* magazine informed its millions of readers, other critics pronounced the play to be "superb," "majestic," "great," and "a play to make history." Luce, stridently pro-capitalist and a foe of FDR, sought to deflate some of the hype, with his magazine's review arguing that such superlatives were "not justified."[142] All the attention bestowed upon Miller promised to make it difficult for him to work in factories or anonymously hang around gin mills anymore.

The bright lights of Broadway success did not alter Miller's left-wing politics, however. Shortly after the play opened, the playwright attended a fundraising dinner for Henry Wallace. Along with *Salesman* producer Bloomgarden and lead actor Cobb, Miller had supported Wallace's presidential bid in 1948 (although Miller was a rising star, Clifford Odets and Lillian Hellman were the

141   Atkinson continued: "Humane in its point of view, [*Salesman*] has stature and insight, awareness of life, respect for people and knowledge of American manners and of modern folkways. From the technical point of view, it is virtuoso theatre." *New York Times* (2-20-1949).

142   *Time* (2-21-1949).

most prominent playwright supporters of the campaign.)
As the *Brooklyn Eagle* noted, joining Miller at the event were
two other "sons of Brooklyn," left-wing lawyers Bernard
Reswick and Leo Linder (who also served as the local
chair of the ALP).[143] Miller's continued support for Wallace
no doubt caught the attention of Luce, a longtime rival of
Wallace. But it didn't stop the *Saturday Evening Post*, which
had similar politics to *Time* while also reaching millions of
readers, from running a long, flattering profile of Miller in
July 1949. As highlighted by journalist Robert Sylvester, the
commercial success of "The Salesman" (as it was known in
the theater business) now promised to make Miller a mil-
lionaire, with Broadway ticket sales, film rights, publishing royalties, and touring productions filling his coffers.[144]
Miller clearly was no longer in the same orbit as the guys in
the factory or middle-class Willy. Early in the play, Linda
Loman assures her anguished husband that "you're doing
wonderful, dear. You're making seventy to a hundred dollars a week." By contrast, Miller and other attendees to the
Wallace fundraiser ponied up $500 a plate.

The star playwright had thus returned to the income
bracket that he had known in his early years, when his
father owned a women's clothing manufacturing company

143 *Brooklyn Eagle* (2-21-1949).

144 Robert Sylvester, "Brooklyn Boy Makes Good," *Saturday Evening Post*
(7-16-1949).

that employed four hundred workers. His family had a chauffeur as well as homes in Harlem and the Rockaways. After the company collapsed one year before the Stock Market crash of 1929, the Millers moved to Midwood, near Ocean Parkway (about two miles from where the Sanders family lived).[145] As the playwright explained to a national audience two decades later, Brooklyn in the early 1930s consisted of many small, insular neighborhoods; Miller described his nook of Midwood "as a village with village crimes," with him and his friends stealing from the candy store or breaking the window of the pharmacy while playing handball.[146] Miller attended Abraham Lincoln High School in Coney Island, graduating in 1932 (the Class of '42 at Lincoln would include the novelist Joseph Heller). As Miller told Sylvester, among his uncles and their many friends who frequented the family's Midwood home were several traveling salesmen. Amidst all the fanfare in the show's opening months, Miller said that he was most proud of the fact that "despite the morbid undertones," the audience often included salesmen attending Manhattan conventions and garment district wholesalers trying to impress their buyers.

---

145   The address of the Miller home was 1350 East Third Street (near Avenue M).

146   Arthur Miller, "A Boy Grew in Brooklyn," *Holiday* (March 1955).

By that summer, Miller had again won the Drama Critics Circle award for best play. Yet as Sylvester noted, the reviewers were not unified in their interpretation of the work's meaning. According to Sylvester, "an important appeal of *The Salesman* is that everyone who sees it finds some personal significance in it, the tragedy of his own or some friend's or relative's life." Although that identification conceivably could derive from Biff or Happy's struggles with their father, or Linda's fruitless efforts to provide emotional support for her troubled husband, Willy remains the central character throughout the entire play. In the estimation of the influential British literary critic Raymond Williams (writing in the late 1950s), "it is not Willy Loman as a man, but the salesman as an image, that predominates." Williams, a Marxist, views that image as the embodiment of "alienation." By this he means that Loman moved "from selling things to selling himself, and has become, in effect, a commodity which like other commodities at a certain point will be economically discarded."[147]Even as the U.S. championed its free enterprise system at the height of the Cold War, the bright lights of Broadway exposed the dark reality of capitalism.

---

147   Raymond Williams, "The Realism of Arthur Miller," from Robert W. Corrigan, ed. *Arthur Miller: A Collection of Critical Essays* (Englewood, NJ: Prentice Hall, 1969), 75. Williams' essay was originally published by the influential British cultural studies journal *Critical Quarterly* in June 1959.

One salesman who was particularly moved by the play was Eli Sanders, father of Larry and Bernie. As Larry recalls, Eli worked for the Keystone Paint & Varnish Company from around the end of the war through his death in 1962. Keystone's factory and offices were located on Otsego Street, just a few short blocks from the Red Hook Houses. In 1947 Keystone gained national notoriety when its paint was used to restore Thomas Jefferson's home at Monticello. Over the next few years its featured products included "odorless" paint, which according to the *Brooklyn Eagle* had provided "a boon to hotels, hospitals, theaters, institutions and private homes." Eli Sanders and other Keystone sales reps also offered a "whiter than white" variety that could be used to make Venetian blinds look brand new. By the mid-1950s, Douglas C. Arnold, the company's president, had become president of the New York State Paint, Varnish and Lacquer Association. As the *Eagle* noted, several of Arnold's employees stayed with the company for decades, with three attaining the thirty-year mark and one reaching fifty-five years at Keystone. Larry Sanders explains that the company's executives "were good to my father, particularly after our mother died, when he fell into a deep depression and couldn't work for a few months. But they kept him on." By contrast, Willy Loman's company had fired him after thirty-four years on the job.[148]

Differences aside, there were plenty of aspects of Loman's life that Eli Sanders could appreciate. Although Willy's product line was never specified, commissions for salesmen in general fluctuated, creating uneven income patterns—and the job thus required constant work. After Linda assures him that he's "doing wonderful" in Act One, Willy replies, "But I gotta be at it ten, twelve hours a day." Such demands could lead to bouts of exhaustion or contribute to depression. Like Willy, Eli had two sons and a wife to provide for, so he could not stop selling paint. As Bernie recalled in his 1997 memoir *Outsider in the House*, his father worked "day after day, year after year." Meanwhile, his mother Dora really wanted "a home of her own," but Eli never managed to attain the same middle-class status[149] as

148 *Brooklyn Eagle* (7-20-1947, 11-30-1949, 4-28-1950, 2-11-50, 5-20-1952, 3-22-1953, and 5-20-1954).

149 A New Deal bank map of Brooklyn from the late 1930s graded Midwood as a "B" in terms of lending, making it one of the more favorable areas for white ethnics to purchase a home. Bay Ridge (then Irish) was the only location in the borough to receive an "A." Most of Flatbush was a "C." The "D"—or redlined—rating was applied to BedStuy and surrounding neighborhoods, where blacks had migrated to during the decade. Large swaths of South Brooklyn, including in and around Coney Island, also received the lowest grade. With a bit more income, Eli Sanders likely could have taken advantage of Midwood's designation to purchase a home. For map, see Emily Badger, "How Redlining's Racist Effects Lasted for Decades," *New York Times* (8-24-2017). For full discussion of redlining in Brooklyn, see Craig Steven Wilder, *A Covenant with Color: Race and Social Power in Brooklyn* (New York: Columbia University Press, 2001), chap. 9.

Willy—or of neighbors on his own block, which also had single-family houses.[150] According to Larry, Eli's sales territory through the mid-1950s was Long Island, which he traversed in the family Plymouth. There, Eli needed to put on a happy face in order to win over housewives, husbands, and business owners, many of whom were Eli's fellow white ethnics who had left Brooklyn for the spacious new suburbs on the Island. Meanwhile, the Sanders family struggled, living in a cramped apartment where Larry and Bernie slept in the living room and the parents frequently fought about money. There's little doubt that Eli and his many contemporaries could see large parts of themselves in Willy. In 2012, Bernie told the *New York Times* that his father reminded him of Willy Loman.[151] As Larry recalls, after seeing *Salesman* on Broadway, Eli Sanders "was shaken up for weeks afterward."

At the time he wrote *Salesman*, Miller was living in Brooklyn Heights, where he had moved in the early 1940s

---

150   Bernie Sanders with Huck Gutman, *Outsider in the House* (New York: Verso Books, 1997), 13. As recently quoted by theorist Ashley Frawley, Marx—in *Wage, Labour and Capital*—observed: "A house may be large or small but as long as the rest of the surrounding houses are likewise small, it satisfies all requirements for a residence. But let there arise next to the house a palace, and the little house shrinks to a hut." https://twitter.com/AshleyAFrawley/status/1226846335195918336?s=20.

151   Sheryl Gay Stolberg, "In the Fiscal Debate, an Unvarnished Voice for Shielding Benefits," *New York Times* (12-13-2012).

while trying to make a living as a writer.[152] After the war ended, as Miller later wrote, he "got interested in the long-shoremen [and] spent a lot of time in Red Hook around Columbia Street," just a few blocks from the Keystone factory.[153] What started as Miller's journalistic interest in mafia control over the waterfront unions became a screenplay completed in 1947 called *The Hook*. Two years after *Salesman* opened on Broadway, Miller and director Elia Kazan traveled to Hollywood to meet with producers interested in the screenplay. On a 20th Century Fox studio lot, Miller first met Marilyn Monroe, and thus began a tempestuous affair that ended Miller's first marriage. According to Miller's foremost biographer Christopher Bigsby, in 1955—soon after she divorced New York Yankees legend Joe DiMaggio—Monroe and Miller went house-hunting in Brooklyn, at one point taking a bicycle

---

152   Miller and his first wife, Mary Slattery, resided at five different Brooklyn Heights addresses through the mid-1950s. They initially lived with roommates at 62 Montague Street before moving to 18 Schermerhorn Street in 1941. In 1944, the Millers moved to a duplex owned by Norman Mailer's parents at 102 Pierrepont Street (where the 1947 Brooklyn Telephone Directory listed their number under Arthur's name as Main 5-2928). After the Broadway success of *All My Sons*, the Millers bought a four-story brownstone at 31 Grace Court that W.E.B. DuBois purchased from the couple in 1951 when they moved to 155 Willow Street. After he took up with Marilyn Monroe in 1955, Arthur left the house to Mary and soon settled in Roxbury, Connecticut, with Marilyn. Helene Stapinski, "Arthur Miller's Brooklyn," *New York Times* (1-24-2016).

153   *Brooklyn Eagle* (2-10-2012).

ride down Ocean Parkway.[154] That purchase never happened, and by mid-decade Miller now called Connecticut home. But the stormy six-year marriage of Broadway's leading playwright and Hollywood's number-one starlet made the duo a regular presence in the New York City gossip pages. Miller's story now became a cautionary tale of the Brooklyn figure who made it big, only to be nearly ruined by fame.[155]

The Hook, meanwhile, shared many connections with *On the Waterfront* (1954). Written by Budd Schulberg and directed by Kazan, the Academy Award-winning drama, though shot in Hoboken, New Jersey, was set on the Red Hook waterfront. Marlon Brando, who had been trained by the Group Theatre's Stella Adler, gives a classic performance as Terry Malloy, a boxer and longshoreman who ultimately rats out mob boss Johnny Friendly, played by *Salesman's* Lee J. Cobb. The story is widely viewed as a defense by Kazan, Schulberg, and Cobb for their friendly testimony to the House Un-American Activities Committee, in which

---

154   Excerpt from Bigsby's 2008 biography in *The Telegraph* (11-16-2008).

155   In 1949, as *Salesman* began to take off, Miller assured the *Times'* Murray Schumach that he had no interest in Hollywood. "I didn't go to Hollywood when I was poor," he noted, contrasting himself with the many writers of his generation who sought work with the studios. Given *Salesman's* success, Miller said, "why should I do it now?" *New York Times* (2-6-1949). Although the film was a box-office flop, Miller's screenplay for *The Misfits* (1961)—which starred Monroe, Clark Gable, and Red Hook-raised Eli Wallach—garnered critical acclaim. One year later, Monroe died from an overdose of barbiturates.

they provided the names of Broadway and Hollywood associates they deemed to have Communist ties. In 1956, Miller, by contrast, testified—but did not name names. Amidst the witch-hunts of the McCarthy era, questions of individual loyalty and political commitment dominated the headlines. *On the Waterfront* was a smash hit at the box-office, with Malloy's most famous line ("I coulda been a contender") becoming a staple phrase of the era's popular culture. The everyday struggles faced by Brooklyn's working class thus remained at the center of postwar American life.

CHAPTER EIGHT:
MERMAID AVENUE

While the docks of Red Hook were Brooklyn's economic center during the mid-twentieth century, Coney Island was its cultural capital. And from the middle of the war through 1950, folk music legend Woody Guthrie lived at 3520 Mermaid Avenue at the western end of the island. The parents of Marjorie Greenblatt, Woody's second wife and mother of their son Arlo (b. 1947) and daughter Nora (b. 1950), lived in nearby Sea Gate. Greenblatt, who later became Marjorie Mazia, was a dancer in Martha Graham's company and she exerted considerable influence over Woody's songwriting during his Coney years. Born in small-town Oklahoma in 1912, Guthrie had moved to the West Coast in the mid-1930s and started appearing on the radio, serving as the radical real-life counterpart to *The Grapes of Wrath*'s Tom Joad. Guthrie first gained widespread national notoriety after the release of *Dust Bowl Ballads*, his debut album, in 1940. During that same year, he also wrote a weekly column called "Woody Sez" in the *People's World,* the Communist Party's West Coast daily newspaper.[156] For a stretch in the early 1940s, Guthrie lived in Greenwich Village with his music partner Pete Seeger, and their music circle included CPUSA-aligned musical figureheads Alan Lomax and Lead Belly. Guthrie's uncompromising politics were famously summed up by the sticker on his guitar that read, "This machine kills fascists."

Even before he set up shop in Coney Island, Guthrie was a known entity in Brooklyn. In October 1942, he and Lead Belly were the headliners for a musical revue slated to open at the Brooklyn Academy of Music (BAM). Titled *It's All Yours,* the work was written by leading left-wing lyricist Earl Robinson, whose song credits included Paul Robeson's "Ballad for the Americans" (included in *Sing for Your Supper,* a WPA/Federal Theatre Project 1939 production) and the labor movement staple "Joe Hill." As the singer prepared to take the stage, the *Brooklyn Eagle's* headline referred to him simply as "Woody, a Steinbeck Discovery." The condescending story portrayed Guthrie upon his arrival in New

---

156   The publication introduced his debut column by referring to Woody as someone who "can tell you about the Dust Bowl, the original characters from *The Grapes of Wrath,* and of the latest letter he got from John Steinbeck." Written in dialect, Guthrie's short initial entry began, "The national debit is one thing I caint figger out. I heard a senator on a radio saying we owed somebody 15 jillion dollars." See https://www.peoplesworld.org/article/woody-guthrie-s-first-daily-worker-column-woody-sez-the-national-debit-is-one-thing-i-caint-figger-out/.

York City a few years prior as an out-of-place "minstrel lad" used to performing at "husking bees" and church picnics. But since then he had performed at trade union halls and at "city-bred folk song festivals." The bumpkin caricature notwithstanding, the *Eagle* accurately conveyed that Woody "knows America" and its "farmers, longshoremen, miners, tenement children, Indians of the desert [and] subway crowds hurrying home from work." Because of a last-minute falling out with the revue's skit writer, Guthrie dropped out of the show at the dress rehearsal. Brooklyn audiences would have other opportunities to see him perform over the next few years, though.[157]

The publication of Guthrie's autobiography *Bound for Glory* in the spring of 1943 garnered Woody significant attention. Writing in the *New Yorker*, the WPA-affiliated popular intellectual Clifton Fadiman heaped praise on both the author and the work. As Fadiman presciently surmised, "Someday people are going to wake up to the fact that Woody Guthrie and the ten thousand songs that leap and tumble off the strings of his music box are a national possession, like Yellowstone and Yosemite, and part of the best stuff this country has to show the world." The reviewer, who had appeared on national radio broadcasts with

---

157   *Brooklyn Eagle* (10-5-1942). Robinson, who was forced to take over Guthrie's role, later wrote "The House I Live In," the song performed by Frank Sinatra in Hollywood director Mervyn LeRoy's anti-bigotry 1945 short film of the same name.

Guthrie, then came down from the mountains to evaluate the book. In Fadiman's view, *Bound for Glory* wouldn't rank among classic autobiographies because it "lacks entirely the element of egotism, even pomposity," that such works possess. The book's unique strength, he said, was its use of dialect, "a language that has the exact speed and timbre of colloquial speech and yet is nervous and alive with metaphor and simile, and musical, too, in a balladlike way."[158] A lifestyle columnist in the *Brooklyn Eagle* who had attended the book party for Guthrie—hosted by the book's publicist, socialite Amy Vanderbilt, at her Madison Avenue home—viewed things differently. *Bound for Glory* in his view was distinguished by its "appallingly bad English [and] hopeless lack of syntax and sentence structure." The prigs lost this battle, however, and Guthrie's book was a critical and commercial success.[159]

After a few years bouncing around the country, Guthrie and Greenblatt had first moved to a small unit above her parents' apartment in Sea Gate in early 1943. In May, as part of its United Nations Concert Series, the Brooklyn Museum hosted Woody, Lead Belly, and Earl Robinson for

158   *New Yorker* (3-20-1943).

159   In his "New York Day by Day" column, the *Eagle*'s man-about-town Charles B. Driscoll observed that Guthrie was "one of the most un-Madison Ave. guests I've seen in many years . . . He was Woody Guthrie of Oklahoma and the wide road, hair uncombed, shirt opened at the top, necktieless, wearing a clean pair of what he calls overalls." *Brooklyn Eagle* (4-5-1943).

a performance of "North American Folk Songs."[160] While Woody was in Europe contributing to the war against fascism via his work in the U.S. Merchant Marine,[161] that fall Marjorie rented a small one-bedroom apartment at 3520 Mermaid Avenue (for $35 per month). After a winter stint on the North African front, then a late spring journey that brought him close to the action at Normandy, Guthrie returned to Coney Island in early August 1944. *The Brooklyn Eagle* soon noted the singer had set up shop there.[162] That fall Guthrie participated in the fight for FDR's reelection while also expressing support for Vito Marcantonio. To drum up support for the president ahead of the November election, Guthrie joined a "Roosevelt Bandwagon" that brought him to Chicago, Minneapolis, Buffalo, and Boston, among other stops. Guthrie was now a national figure with a strong local following, as illustrated by his Sunday afternoon radio program that debuted in December 1944 on WNEW, a Newark, New Jersey-based station best known for helping launch Frank Sinatra's career. In 1934, FDR had thrown the switch that brought the station on the air. But Guthrie's show only lasted a few

---

160   *Brooklyn Eagle* (5-14-1943).

161   Guthrie mainly worked in the kitchens of cargo ships but on a few occasions Axis torpedoes nearly killed him. See Joe Klein, *Woody Guthrie: A Life* (New York: Random House, 1999 ed.), 276–282.

162   *Brooklyn Eagle* (9-18-1944).

months, presumably because the radicalism of the song he wrote for the program called "When I Get Home"—which envisioned vets returning to an integrated America with strong labor unions—was not what WNEW's executives wanted to hear.[163]

As the war entered its final year, Guthrie became a fixture on the streets and barstools of Coney Island. In September 1944, a *Brooklyn Eagle* columnist referred to Guthrie as "the Oklahoman who became an Ourtowner," adding that the singer was one local who "doesn't seem to give a darn about money."[164] The acclaimed troubadour author was not hard to find. Despite his fame, he was listed in the 1947 Brooklyn Telephone Directory with his Mermaid Avenue address and number: Esplanade 2–5751.[165] (By contrast, after the success of *All My Sons*, Arthur Miller no longer listed his number in the book.) During the seven-year stretch that he called Mermaid Avenue home, Woody was quite prolific, writing dozens of songs. Some looked to the past for inspiration. In "Harriet Tubman's Ballad" (1944), Woody summoned the ghosts of

---

163 Klein, *Woody Guthrie*, 292-300. For WNEW's history, see http://www.metromediaradio.net/online-jazz-music-metromedia-radio/legacy-wnew-1130-am-history/.

164 *Brooklyn Eagle* (9-19-1944).

165 The telephone exchange system at the time used the first two letters to connect to a service area. The word was used in order to help customers remember the letters.

nineteenth-century radicals including Tubman and John Brown. Others addressed Guthrie's immediate surroundings. As he watched ships pass by Coney, Woody wrote several songs making references to voyages at sea. And he closely observed everyday urban life. In "My New York City" (1947), he wrote that "I've walked and rode in rain and sun through Brooklyn, Bronx and Queens," with a line in the chorus reading, "Walk our beach sand and our blades of green grass." In style and substance, Guthrie's democratic reverie paid homage to Walt Whitman, Brooklyn's literary pioneer.[166]

Like many of his artistic peers, Woody also continued to play an active role in local political organizing after the war. In March 1946, the Bensonhurst chapter of the CPUSA-affiliated International Workers Order held a fundraiser for Russian relief efforts that featured Guthrie.[167] Three months later, Brooklyn's chapter of the American Labor Party held a two-day organizing event at the Biltmore Hall in Flatbush. The bazaar featured folk dances and gift items

---

166 For a complete list of songs Guthrie wrote while living at Coney, see https://www.woodyguthrie.org/WGWay.htm (lyrics also available on same site.) Guthrie also wrote "Walt Whitman's Niece," which became the opening track on *Mermaid Avenue*, Billy Bragg and Wilco's critically acclaimed 1998 album that put the lyrics Woody wrote during his Coney years to music.

167 *Brooklyn Eagle* (3-18-1956). Formed in 1930, the I.W.O. was best known for providing low-cost insurance to its 200,000 members. Under attack during the Cold War, the group dissolved in 1954.

for sale contributed by the ALP's thirty political clubs in Brooklyn. Headlining the first night's entertainment was Arthur Miller, who had gained notoriety as a result of his 1945 novel *Focus*, which dealt with wartime anti-Semitism (including that of the Flatbush-based Christian Front). On the second night, Guthrie performed along with a troupe of folk dancers. Miller and Guthrie also soon shared a mutual friend in Vincent J. Longhi, better known as "Jimmy." Longhi, a labor attorney, introduced Miller to some of his longshoremen's union clients on the Red Hook docks, which Miller later said provided the basis of his screenplay *The Hook.* In the fall of 1946, Woody helped his Merchant Marine comrade Jimmy campaign for Congress on the ALP line. The waterfront district spanned from Red Hook through Gowanus (and what's currently considered South Park Slope and Sunset Park) to Borough Park. Rather than endorse the Democratic incumbent, John J. Rooney, the ALP supported Longhi, who—following the examples of La Guardia and Vito Marcantonio—also ran as a Republican.

First elected to Congress in 1944 with ALP support, Rooney quickly became an outspoken anti-Communist, thus spurring the left's interest in unseating him. Rooney was backed by the party machine but also had powerful friends in Washington. In late October, the *Brooklyn Eagle* ran a two-part series detailing the extensive participation of Longhi (1916–2006) in Communist Party activities dating back to 1934. As the *Eagle* (a Democratic Party organ) explained at the outset of its lead Sunday story, a conspicuously named "Non-Partisan Veterans Committee" supporting Rooney had provided the research on his leftist opponent. That information, the story noted, came from "unidentified 'official government files.'" Rooney was later known to have close ties to FBI Director J. Edgar Hoover, and the depth of the research certainly suggested that it was the bureau's handiwork. In addition to a CPUSA nominating petition he had signed in 1942, the *Eagle* highlighted the various articles Longhi had written in *L'Unita del Popolo*, the New York City publication for Italian Communists. Pete Cacchione, Brooklyn's Communist City Councilman, was the paper's other "star writer," the *Eagle* asserted. The second installment continued with the innuendo, questioning Longhi's residency in Brooklyn as well as whether he was misrepresenting his wartime record (which Longhi refuted by noting that New York's highest court had ruled that the Merchant Marine qualified as service in the "armed forces"). The smear campaign notwithstanding, Governor Dewey and the Republican Party—sensing the opportunity to steal a seat from the Democrats, who held all of Brooklyn's congressional offices—stood firmly behind Longhi.[168]

---

168   *Brooklyn Eagle* (10-27-1946 and 10-28-46). Rooney's ties to Hoover
       mentioned in *New York Times* obituary (10-28-75).

Longhi ran what the *New York Times* characterized at the time as a "spectacular campaign."[169] Woody and his longtime music partner Cisco Houston performed on a flatbed truck for longshoremen on the Red Hook docks.[170] But Woody wasn't the only musical icon of the period who got behind Longhi's bid. A loudspeaker on Guthrie's flatbed delivered the following statement:

This is Frank Sinatra, speaking to you as a citizen. I envy the people of Brooklyn [because of] their chance to send Vincent J. Longhi to Congress. Jim Longhi is a man who [has] spent most of his life fighting bigotry and race hatred. That's why if I were in Brooklyn now, I'd be campaigning for him. And there are other reasons to elect him, too. Jim doesn't just talk about health clinics and playgrounds for children, and decent wages for all the people. These things are not just topics for campaign speeches for him. These are things closest to his heart. He has plans, real plans for bringing them about. That's why I sincerely hope that the people of Red Hook, Borough Park and the Gowanus District will send him to Congress, as I believe that Brooklyn and the rest of the country will be mighty proud of Vincent J. Longhi.[171]

---

169   *New York Times* (11-3-1946).

170   Klein, *Woody Guthrie*, 342.

171   Sinatra recording available here: https://www.youtube.com/watch?v=Y-d1OKRvzaIo. In reporting Sinatra's endorsement, *The Brooklyn Eagle* (11-3-1946) noted that the statement also included the lines "[Longhi] is a square shooter, a fighter, the kind of man I'd like my boy to grow up to be."

In plugging Longhi (the singer's cousin),[172] Sinatra sounded like he was talking about La Guardia. The Little Flower had proven that such a socially benevolent agenda could be enacted. But in the eyes of the local Democratic machine and its allies, Longhi and the ALP were insurgent reds encroaching on their turf.

Despite escalating Cold War hostilities, the candidate backed by Republicans and Communists nearly prevailed on the Brooklyn waterfront. Illustrating the rising tide of anti-Communism, both *PM* and the *New York Post* endorsed the machine Democrat rather than the left-wing challenger. Longhi nonetheless lost to Rooney by only 5,500 votes. The challenger tallied 24,000 on the Republican line along with nearly 6,900 from ALP supporters. Just over 110,000 ALP votes were cast throughout Brooklyn (out of 272,000 citywide), and ALP-supported candidates won seven of the borough's nine seats in Congress, in all cases when the party backed the Democrat. In the Sanders family's congressional district, Democrat Leo Rayfiel cruised to reelection with over 75 percent support; in the assembly district where both Rayfiel and the Sanders family resided,[173] Rayfiel received over 12,200 votes on the

172   *Daily News* (10-4-1946). Family ties to Longhi notwithstanding, Sinatra was fully aligned with the left during this period.

173   Because the paper viewed it as "increasingly important [for readers] to communicate with their Representatives," the *Brooklyn Eagle* (2-12-1946) printed the home addresses of Rayfiel and his colleagues

ALP line (roughly 30 percent of his total). Thus, although Longhi's bid failed, the ALP appeared to be a growing force in Brooklyn.[174]

Woody continued to be active in left-wing political campaigns over the next few years. In November 1947, the Theatre Arts Committee of Brooklyn's ALP chapter promoted "Music in a Democratic Key," a five-event series slated for BAM spread across the next few months. The third event, scheduled for January, promised to feature Paul Robeson, and the headliners for the following month's event would be Woody and Alan Lomax (who in addition to his work as a musicologist also played the guitar). Titled "Songs for Mr. Lincoln," Guthrie's performance was slated for the night before Honest Abe's birthday.[175] The series appears to have been cancelled, once more depriving BAM audiences of the chance to see Woody. But along with Arthur Miller and Robeson, Guthrie was active on the ALP's political trail throughout the year. People's Songs, a folk music organization started in 1944 by Pete Seeger and

earlier in the year. Rayfield lived at 1818 Avenue L in Midwood and Rooney resided at 217 Congress St. in Cobble Hill, next to Red Hook.

174   Vote totals in *Brooklyn Eagle* (11-6-1946). Longhi ran again in 1948 but only on the ALP line and thus got crushed, although he again tallied 7,000 ALP votes (two years later, he got about half that total). Rooney held the seat in Congress through his retirement in 1974. In a scandal-ridden 1972 campaign, the leading Vietnam War critic Allard Lowenstein nearly toppled him.

175   *Brooklyn Eagle* (11-16-1947).

Lomax, recruited Woody and Cisco to perform at Henry Wallace presidential campaign events throughout the summer and fall of 1948. The CPUSA was an ally of People's Songs and a driving force in Wallace's campaign. Guthrie participated because he hated Truman, explaining that the Cold War Democrat "don't like organized labor, don't like the Communist Party, don't like the human race." He was also upset that Eleanor Roosevelt lent her powerful endorsement to Truman. In "Dear Mrs. Roosevelt" (1948), Woody's lyrics included positive references to the fact that FDR had "[s]hook hands with Joseph Stalin," a far different approach than Truman's. In "Henry Wallace Man" (1948), Guthrie praised the candidate for seeking "peace with Russians." Although he composed several new songs and reworked lyrics from his older ones, Guthrie didn't like the "agit-prop" components of his People's Song colleagues, including Lomax.[176]

During his Coney Island years, Woody became familiar with Brooklyn's rich Jewish folklore and heritage. Aliza Greenblatt, Marjorie's mother, was a leading Yiddish poet of the mid-twentieth century whose words were often set to music. Woody, raised Protestant but not practicing at

---

176 Guthrie's Truman statement and his lyrics for Roosevelt and Wallace songs quoted in Will Kaufman, *Woody Guthrie: American Radical (Urbana, IL: University of Illinois Press, 2011)*, 134–142. "Agit-prop" was a term used by folk musician Bess Lomax Hawes (Alan Lomax's sister) to describe Woody's views. See Ed Cray, *Ramblin' Man: The Life and Times of Woody Guthrie* (New York: W.W. Norton, 2004), 327–328.

the time, embraced Jewish culture, particularly the celebration of Hanukah. In 1949, he wrote seven holiday songs, which is somewhat surprising given that as he noted—in "Happy Joyous Hanuka"—there are eight days of the event. Some of Guthrie's compositions fused Okie square dance repetitions with Jewish tradition. As "Hanukah Tree" began, "Round and round my Hanukah tree/Round and round I go." And they also included Woody's cross-cultural wordplay. "Hanuka Dance," for example, includes references to dance partners as latkes and strudel. Not all of Woody's reflections on Jewish culture during the period were so upbeat, however. His first-person ballad of "Ilsa Koch" (1948) began in Buchenwald and included vivid descriptions of the death camp. Taken as a whole, Guthrie's songs showed a clear appreciation for the resilience of Brooklyn's Jewish culture in the aftermath of the Holocaust. In turn, two leading Jewish folk musicians of the next few decades—Woody's protégé Ramblin' Jack Elliott (born Elliot Adnopoz in 1931 and raised in Midwood) and his son Arlo—would honor Guthrie's heartland roots.[177]

Although he never recorded them, Guthrie wrote lyrics for two songs that portrayed Coney Island as a place that contained both joy and struggle. In "Coney Coney"

---

177   Lyrics at WoodyGuthrie.org. At the suggestion of Marjorie and Woody's
        daughter Nora, the Klezmatics set Woody's words to klezmer music in
        the early 2000s.

(1947), he explored the relationship of a man and a woman, stating "I'm married and wed to a dancer" and later naming Marjorie. Guthrie exhorts her to "Dance out" of their home to "see fighting," "run factories," and "to sing equal." And "if your man keeps your Heart tied," he says, "dance out and untie it."[178] In Guthrie's view, the fight for women's equality indeed began at home. In "Mermaid's Avenue" (1950), Guthrie mixed descriptions of summertime fun with references to class conflict. He rhapsodized about Coney as a place "where all colors of goodfolks meet," as evidenced by the blintzes, "hot Mexican Chili," and chop suey fare available on and around the boardwalk. But the section at the west end of the beach where his in-laws lived was far less welcoming. At Sea Gate, he wrote, there were "cops to stop you" and "bulls [aka security guards] along that wire fence/Scare the mermaids all away."[179] As the masses reveled in the summertime fun, the middle class of the Coney area retreated to a gated community. There was little doubt which side of the fence Woody preferred.

Guthrie soon observed firsthand that despite its inviting summertime atmosphere, Coney Island was also a residentially segregated place. In December 1950, Woody, Marjorie, Arlo, and Nora moved from Mermaid Avenue to

---

178   For lyrics, see Nora Guthrie, *My Name is New York: Ramblin' Around Woody Guthrie's Town* (Brooklyn, NY: powerHouse Books, 2014), 63.

179   Lyrics at WoodyGuthrie.org.

the Beach Haven apartment complex across from Coney Island Hospital. The family's two-bedroom unit with a large balcony rented for $120 per month. Woody soon realized that all of his neighbors were white, a fact he attributed to the discriminatory practice of his landlord, Fred Trump, who built several similar complexes in the area. A few years later, Guthrie jotted down notes and lyrics in his notebooks, under various headings including "Beach Haven Race Hate," "Beach Haven Ain't My Home," and "Old Man Trump."[180] One poem verse begins:

I suppose
Old Man Trump
Knows just how much
He stirred up
In the bloodpot of human hearts
When he drawed
That color line.

Even as he and his family now enjoyed their spacious modern dwelling, Woody felt uneasy about contributing to his racist landlord's bank account. Reworking lyrics from his Dust Bowl ballad "I Ain't Got No Home," Guthrie continued:

Beach Haven ain't my home!
I just cain't pay this rent!

180 Amanda Petrusich, "A Story about Fred Trump and Woody Guthrie for the Midterm Elections," *New Yorker* (11-6-2018).

My money is down the drain!
And my soul is badly spent!
Beach Haven looks like heaven
Where no black ones come to roam
No, no, no! Old Man Trump!
Old Beach Haven ain't my home![181]

The son of a Klansman, Woody had been crusading against racism since he first came onto the scene in the late 1930s. He didn't stay long in Trump's complex, although the reasons were more personal than political. Woody's marriage with Marjorie was falling apart, and he began to experience health problems. Guthrie left Brooklyn in the fall of 1952, and the next times he returned for extended stays—1954–1956 and 1961–1966—he resided in a psychiatric institution then called Brooklyn State Hospital in East Flatbush.

The Sanders family lived just five stops on the Brighton Beach Line from Kings Highway to Coney Island. Like the Greenblatts and many thousands of other families in the area, the Sanders were proud of their Jewish heritage. According to Larry, they mostly kept kosher at home. The family attended the Kingsway Jewish Center on Kings

---

181   Verses from Will Kaufman, "Woody Guthrie, 'Old Man Trump,' and a Real Estate Empire's Racist Foundations," *The Conversation* (1-21-2016); and "In Another Newly Discovered Song, Woody Guthrie Continues His Assault on 'Old Man Trump'," *The Conversation* (9-5-2016). Kaufman discovered Woody's notes about Trump at the Guthrie Center in Tulsa, Oklahoma.

Highway and Nostrand, and there Larry and Bernie each attended Hebrew school on the weekends ahead of their Bar Mitzvahs. According to Bernie's high school and college friend Steve Slavin, Bernie and his pals later would regularly sneak into the Center in order to play basketball in the basement. The common geography between the Sanders and Guthrie families meant that from their roof, Larry and Bernie also had a good view of the July Fourth fireworks at Coney Island. Although they preferred to swim at adjacent Brighton Beach, the Sanders brothers frequented the boardwalk and amusements at Coney in the summers during the 1950s.[182]

As Larry recalls, around 1950–1951, after he first started working at various jobs as a teenager, he purchased a record player. Among the first albums he remembers owning were those of Lead Belly put out on the seminal Folkways label, which debuted in 1950. Born in Poland in 1905, Folkways producer Moses Asch was the son of Sholem Asch, a prominent Yiddish novelist. After leaving Poland during World War I, the family settled in New York City, with Moses spending part of his youth in Brooklyn. After launching his earlier label Asch Records in 1941 (that featured Lead Belly), Asch was introduced to Guthrie by

182   The Sanders family also shared the same telephone exchange with the
      Guthries, with the former reachable at Esplanade 7-3553.

Alan Lomax.[183] In 1950, Folkways issued its first Guthrie platter, *Talking Dust Bowl* (which featured "Tom Joad," a two-part ballad). Larry Sanders doesn't remember at what age Bernie first heard Guthrie but says it was "early on" in his brother's life that Bernie first took a liking to Guthrie, as well as to Pete Seeger and Irish Folk Songs; he also appreciated Beethoven's violin concerto. Eli Sanders, says Larry, was more traditional, preferring the music of Yossele Rosenblatt, a popular Ukrainian cantor (or singer of liturgy) whose work was available on Columbia Records.

It was in 1952 that Guthrie's "This Land Is Your Land" was first heard widely, after Folkways made it the title track of a collection that also included songs from Seeger, Lead Belly, and Cisco Houston. Woody had first written it while living in Greenwich Village in 1940 as a response to Irving Berlin's sappy "God Bless America," which was playing constantly on the radio during the build-up to the U.S. entry to the war. His initial recording of it, in 1944, was not released until the Smithsonian unearthed it in the 1990s. But while he was living on Mermaid Avenue, Woody included the lyrics to what he then called simply "This

---

183   Gene Bluestein, "Moses Asch, Documentor," *American Music* (Fall 1987), 302. In the same oral history, Asch explains that during WWI his family first lived in the Bronx, then Brooklyn, before moving to Staten Island, where he attended high school. Asch also told Bluestein that Woody distrusted him because he didn't like "middle-class, bourgeois people." The folk singer preferred to sit on the floor of the record executive's office.

Land" in a self-published 1945 pamphlet that included his home address. Selling for twenty-five cents, the song book was mostly typed (albeit with plenty of hand-corrected mistakes) and included Woody's scribbles and doodles. It also presented his updated motto: "Fascism fought indoors and out/Good weather or bad/Full or empty halls." Woody's introductory statement included many similarly rousing comments. "In these ten songs," he began, "you will hear a lot of music of a lot of races. Songs of every color." He viewed the works as "singing history," a diary of the "blood, sweat, work and tears [and of] slums, bad housing...[and] our fight to have unions and free speech and a family of nations." Woody offered some choice words for his mortal enemies. "[W]e'll burn his soul in hell," he said regarding Hitler. Meanwhile, "Jim Crow and fascism are one and the same."[184]

Guthrie also expressed confidence in the potential of "This Land" to motivate the masses. Referring to it in his pamphlet as "This Land Was Made for You and Me," Woody declared that "[t]he main thing about this song is, you think about these Eight words all the rest of your life and they'll come a bubbling up into Eighty Jillion all Union. Try it and see." After the eponymous 1952 collection

---

184   "Ten Songs of Woody Guthrie" (1945). See Pamphlet available
      via Electronic Frontier Foundation: https://www.eff.org/document/
      ten-songs-woody-guthrie-1945-pamphlet.

brought it widespread notoriety, "This Land" was included four years later on Folkways' platter *Bound for Glory: The Songs and Story of Woody Guthrie*, which also featured the popular actor Will Geer (a pivotal figure in Woody's career) reading passages of the singer's autobiography. Here it was titled "This Is Your Land." Later in the decade, a depoliticized version of what was now commonly called "This Land Is Your Land" was performed by the Kingston Trio and other pop-folk acts. By the early 1960s, it was a staple on the folk circuit that supported the Civil Rights Movement.[185] Throughout the decade versions of it would be recorded by political performers including Peter, Paul and Mary and Woody's pal Pete Seeger. TV footage from the early 1960s showed that youthful audiences knew the chorus and sang along.[186] Through his years as mayor of Burlington, Vermont to his first run for president, the folk anthem Woody Guthrie distributed from Mermaid Avenue would remain a staple on the soundtrack of Bernie's political career.

185   For a history of the song's various audiences from the mid-1950s through 2010, see Kaufman, *Woody Guthrie*, 191–92 and 200–203.

186   See Mexican-American pop-folk singer Trini Lopez perform it in December 1963: https://www.youtube.com/watch?v=Vx8qFhbLsmk.

CHAPTER NINE:
COLD WAR BROOKLYN

At mid-century, the New Deal was alive and well in New York City, although it was managed by a figure far less personable than La Guardia or O'Dwyer. No longer content in his second-fiddle role, Robert Moses now became the conductor. After the war he began to face increasingly vocal opposition to his various projects, magnifying his legendary disdain for any and all opposition. "Critics build nothing," he famously said—and when legendary foe Jane Jacobs helped lead the fight in the late 1950s that stopped the master builder's plan to extend 5th Avenue through Washington Square, he derisively called her a "housewife." Throughout the 1940s, although it was a privately owned project, the massive, racially exclusive Stuyvesant Town rental complex on Manhattan's East Side had received considerable logistical support from Moses. As shown by historian Martha Biondi, after the complex opened in 1947, Communists and their allies stood at the forefront of the opposition. Along with Democrats, Republicans, and members of the Liberal Party and American Labor Party, Communists formed a large tenants committee demanding integration. As seen in his response to Jackie Robinson's criticisms in 1949, over the next few years Paul Robeson helped keep the spotlight on the racist practices of the Metropolitan Life Insurance Company, which owned Stuyvesant Town. In 1950, tenant committee chair Paul Ross, a former La Guardia administration rent commissioner and the ALP's candidate in the mayoral special election that year, sued the city on behalf of black tenants. Of the many daily newspapers, only the liberal *New York Post* supported the integrationist efforts. The pressure achieved only token success, and even after the City Council outlawed discrimination at Stuyvesant Town in 1951, de facto exclusion remained in place through the remainder of the decade and beyond. But the left had helped set in motion the sea change in public opinion Moses would experience through the '50s and '60s.[187]

At the same time as the Stuyvesant fight, the ALP and fellow travelers led a citywide campaign on behalf of nearly all renters in the city. The federal government had established rent control in 1943 but those protections were set to expire in 1950. After the war, left-wing activists created tenant councils in order to advocate for renters. Brooklyn

---

187   Biondi, 127–134.

saw the growth of eighteen such groups, mainly in Jewish neighborhoods, which had many renters as well as strong pockets of ALP and Communist support; in addition to large councils in Brownsville and Borough Park, there were several smaller ones in the greater Flatbush area where the Sanders family lived. During his mayoral bid, the ALP's Paul Ross called attention to the landlord-friendly policies of Moses and the O'Dwyer, then Impellitteri, administrations. In the topsy-turvy era of New York politics, it was the Republican governor Dewey who in an election year (1950) pushed through permanent rent control protections that covered both New York City and the rest of the state. As seen at Stuyvesant Town, the Democrats were tied to the city's large landlords. Labor activists, Communists and the party of big business thus successfully joined together to ensure that working and lower-middle-class families like Bernie's could have secure housing.[188] During both of his presidential campaigns, Bernie's recollections about his childhood in Brooklyn have frequently highlighted the fact that rent control helped ensure his family's stability.

188   Joel Schwartz, "Tenant Power in the Liberal City, 1943–1971," in Ronald Lawson (with Mark Naison), ed., *The Tenant Movement in New York City, 1904–1984* (New Brunswick, NJ: Rutgers University Press, 1986), 137–153. In October 1950, Dewey blasted an NYC system of rent control created by the O'Dwyer administration as rife with the "stench" of "Tammany crookedness." The state's rent control laws replaced the city's version. *New York Times* (10-21-1950). The current system, called rent stabilization, took shape in 1962.

The Sanders family was not a union household, nor was Eli working in a blue-collar profession. But as the rent control campaign illustrated, the achievements of labor activists had widespread benefits for working people across the city. In addition to housing security, non-union families also benefitted from the low-cost health care system established in New York City during the period. While individual unions established health centers that served their own members, in 1944 the La Guardia administration had created the Health Insurance Plan (HIP) of Greater New York, which covered municipal workers and allowed private employers to join. In *Working-Class New York*, labor historian Joshua Freeman states that "by the late 1950s, roughly a million New Yorkers got some of their health care through a union clinic or HIP." Even more common was the Blue Cross network, the vast expansion of which during the period resulted from union participation. As Larry Sanders recalls, Keystone Paints provided Eli Sanders what was then called "hospital insurance" that covered the household (akin to what is now called major medical).[189] Although there was no universal system during the period, affordable health care was a reality for

---

189   As Bernie's high-school pal Myron Kalin explains, during the 1950s primary care doctors along Kings Highway in Midwood charged $3–$7 max per office visit; doctors making house calls charged $5–$10. An *Eagle* classified ad stated in February 1954 that $50 was a typical weekly starting salary for salesmen (plus commission).

many working-class families in Brooklyn and across the city.[190]

Whether members of union families or not, every New York City resident during the 1950s could attest to the power of organized labor because of frequent strikes and related work stoppages. Residents across the city frequently confronted the threat of potential transit strikes, and in Brooklyn, workers often shut down the port. In January 1953, both stoppages happened simultaneously, as 8,200 city bus drivers in the Transport Workers Union, led by combative Mike Quill (a former ally of the CPUSA), went out at the same time as the International Longshoremen's Association. The docks were partially reopened on the first weekend of the year, but the bus stoppage jammed the subways, leaving countless numbers of workers, students and others scrambling to get around for the next several days. In October, the ILA again shut down the waterfront and a few weeks later, the city's milk delivery drivers commenced a weeklong work stoppage. According to the *Brooklyn Eagle*, the disruption of fresh milk supplies affected no less than 12 million people in the metropolitan area. In late November, twenty thousand newspaper workers went out, including those at the *New York Post* and *New York Times*. And in early December, Quill threatened

190   Freeman, 125–131.

another year-end walkout. Such displays of labor militancy provided a clear demonstration of who ran the city.[191]

Bernie's experience in Brooklyn during his adolescence matched many of his peers. Common street games—whether stickball, stoopball, etc.—were a favorite pastime. As Bernie explained to a CBS reporter in 2016, the various activities with neighborhood kids also taught him "a very important lesson about democracy. We didn't have much adult supervision . . . so we worked out our own rules."[192] On Saturday mornings, he and Larry went to see matinees at the Nostrand, their local theater on Kings Highway that often screened cartoons for kids.[193] When he reached his early teens, Bernie started going away to summer camp. Located in the southern Catskills near the Pennsylvania border, the Ten Mile River Scout Camp has a distinguished history. Prior to his election as governor of New York in 1928, FDR had served as president of the New York City Boy Scout Foundation. And it was FDR who selected the 12,000-acre Ten Mile River site. Bernie's predecessors included an eclectic array of influential figures,

---

191   *Brooklyn Eagle* (1-2-1953, 1-5-1953, 10-6-1953, 10-23-1953, 11-30-1953 and 12-3-1953).

192   "Bernie Sanders Goes Back to Brooklyn," CBS News (2-10-2016). Go to: https://www.cbsnews.com/news/campaign-2016-bernie-sanders-goes-back-to-brooklyn/.

193   Brooklyn then had dozens of neighborhood movie theaters. Many, like the Nostrand, have been torn down; others have been repurposed as mini-department stores.

including Latin music legend Tito Puente (1923–2000, raised in Spanish Harlem), Bronx-reared actor Tony Curtis (né Bernard Schwartz, 1925–2000) and Supreme Court judge Antonin Scalia (1936–2016, who grew up in Elmhurst, Queens). The summer camp provided teen boys the opportunity to develop their athletic and leadership skills in a rustic setting far from the crowded, sweltering city. Boy Scout Bernie loved attending Ten Mile, later telling the *New York Times* that he used to "cry on the bus" that brought him home as the camp ended.[194]

Though it remained overwhelmingly Democratic, Brooklyn's support for the party's presidential candidate was not a given in the 1950s. In his two losses to Eisenhower, Adlai Stevenson tried to mobilize support from Eleanor Roosevelt's loyal base of supporters in the borough. Amid the Korean War, Stevenson, then governor of Illinois, challenged Ike in 1952 as a peace candidate who adhered to the UN blueprint for international cooperation and touted his support for the New Deal. As Eleanor told readers of her widely syndicated "My Day" column in late October 1952, "I think the overriding concern about peace, and about preserving the well-being that the people now enjoy in this country, will make them vote for Governor

---

194 For a history of the camp, see Ian Pugh, "Ten Mile River Scout Camps Host Alumni Weekend," *River Reporter* (8-2-2017). For Bernie's recollection, see Mark Leibovich, "The Socialist Senator," *New York Times Magazine* (1-21-2007).

Stevenson."[195] As Election Day approached, Stevenson made a high-profile visit to Brooklyn. Taking a cue from Truman's triumphant 1948 campaign tour, Stevenson addressed 3,000 supporters at Williamsburg Bridge Plaza, then went via motorcade through Clinton Hill and Fort Greene to BAM. The Democratic hopeful's Friday night address was broadcast live on both TV and radio across the nation. An overflow crowd of 3,500 also heard the candidate critique General Eisenhower's positions on the war in Korea. "Adlai Sees Boro Landslide," read the *Brooklyn Eagle*'s headline, with Democratic leaders confidently forecasting that Stevenson could count on a margin of 350,000 votes in the borough. When the returns came in, Ike prevailed easily, winning both nationally and in New York State by 55–44 percent. Although Brooklyn provided only 210,000 more ballots for Stevenson than Ike, just over one-quarter came from the Sanders family's district, where Eleanor's man Adlai won easily.[196]

Roosevelt and her allies next aimed to reassert their influence in New York City politics. During his first full term, Impellitteri had initiated several revenue-raising measures—including an increase in the subway fare (from ten to fifteen cents) and hike in the sales tax—that made

195   Eleanor Roosevelt, "My Day" (10-24-52). See: https://www2.gwu. edu/~erpapers/myday/displaydoc.cfm?_y=1952&_f=md002361.

196   *Brooklyn Eagle* (11-1-1948 and 11-5-1948).

him unpopular. Along with Senator Herbert Lehman, Eleanor lent support to the "New Deal-Fair Deal" wing of the state Democratic Party, which included Robert F. Wagner Jr., then Manhattan borough president. In September 1953, Wagner dispatched Impellitteri in the Democratic primary by a nearly 2–1 margin. Even though the Brooklyn Democratic machine backed the incumbent mayor (who no longer used the Experience Party line), Wagner received nearly 60 percent in the borough. In the Sanders family's district, the challenger prevailed by over 3–1. Wagner then cruised to victory in a three-way race in the November general election, defeating a Republican and a Liberal Party challenger. Wagner took Midwood, but the Liberal Party's candidate, Rudolph Halley, who had been city council president, came within three thousand votes in the district. Wagner had nonetheless recaptured City Hall for the New Dealers, who next turned their sights to Albany.[197]

Meanwhile, the Red Scare reached a fever pitch during Ike's first term. In June 1953, Ethel and Julius Rosenberg went to the electric chair at Sing Sing after their convictions two years earlier for selling atomic secrets to the Soviet Union. Though the couple had been widely vilified in the press, the *New York Post* played a particularly pivotal role

---

197 *New York Times* (9-16-1954) and *Brooklyn Eagle* (11-4-1954).

in shaping negative opinion about the Rosenbergs.[198] After their execution, an Orthodox Jewish funeral was held for both Ethel and Julius on Church Avenue in Brownsville, with hundreds of people coming to pay their respects. The Manhattan couple was then buried at Wellwood, a Jewish cemetery in West Babylon on Long Island; among the speakers at the gravesite was W.E.B. DuBois. Two days after the execution, the magazine section of the *New York Post*'s Sunday edition featured two lengthy recaps of the case. Although both portrayed the couple as Soviet dupes, the second story—by veteran journalist George Trow— showed sensitivity to the impact of the execution on the Rosenbergs' two adolescent sons.[199]

The following spring, Republican senator Joseph McCarthy of Wisconsin brought his anti-Communist inquisition into American living rooms in televised hearings that tried to highlight alleged Red infiltration of the U.S. Army. Among the leading participants in both the Rosenberg case and Army-McCarthy hearings was the senator's chief counsel Roy Cohn. Though only twenty-four at the time, the Bronx-raised Cohn prosecuted

---

198 In their influential 1965 work *Invitation to an Inquest*, which first cast doubt on the Rosenbergs' guilt, Walter and Miriam Schneir cite several moments in the case when key interviews or information first turned up in the *Post*.

199 *New York Post* (6-21-1953). Trow's son, George W.S. Trow, became a *New Yorker* mainstay starting in the mid-1960s.

the Rosenbergs as an assistant U.S. attorney; the notorious fixer enjoyed a close relationship with Judge Irving Kaufman, a fellow Jewish anti-Communist, who sentenced the duo to death. McCarthy's fateful showdown with the army—an institution at the height of its public standing—had been driven by Cohn's effort to carve out special treatment for his presumed lover David Schine, who had been drafted in 1953. (The *New York Post* was far more critical of McCarthy than most newspapers, causing McCarthy and Cohn to wage a smear campaign against its editor, James Wechsler.)[200] As the mid-term elections approached, Eisenhower's hands-off approach to the egregious antics of McCarthy and Cohn made him appear weak and vulnerable.

In late October 1954, Stevenson came back to Brooklyn in order to stump for Eleanor and company's New Deal slate in the New York statewide races—and this time he landed three blocks from the Sanders family's home at P.S. 197, the grade school Larry and Bernie attended. In his 1997 memoir, Bernie explained that his parents "went to only one political meeting that I can recall, when Adlai Stevenson spoke at my elementary school, P.S. 197." Bernie and his folks attended what the *New York Post* described as a "tumultuous rally," joining one thousand fellow Democratic loyalists who

---

200   Nicholas von Hoffman, *Citizen Cohn: The Life and Times of Roy Cohn* (New York: Doubleday, 1988), 98–102 and 178–180.

were "yelling themselves hoarse" and "wielding cowbells." Outside, an additional one thousand Stevenson enthusiasts gathered to listen to the proceedings via loudspeakers. Stevenson was there to express support for Averell Harriman, a former Truman cabinet member now running for governor; and FDR Jr., a member of Congress (representing Manhattan's Upper West Side) but now running for attorney general. As the *Post* noted, Stevenson's address focused on national rather than local issues. He accused the Eisenhower administration of "giveaways" to favored business interests. "From taxes to atomic energy," Adlai declared, and "from oil to timber to grazing lands," the Republicans had shown "a vigorous consistency in transferring from the many to the few." More than six decades later, Bernie would echo that critique at his own raucous rallies in Brooklyn and across the nation.[201]

With Eleanor cheering him on, FDR Jr. waged a spirited campaign for attorney general. In early October, he had received a warm welcome on a Sunday tour of Brooklyn. Considered a more handsome, albeit less politically gifted version of his father, the "glamor boy"—as the *Brooklyn Eagle* called him—kissed women's hands on the Coney Island boardwalk and waved to large cheering crowds in Flatbush, Brownsville, and Bed-Stuy. According to the

New York Times, "impromptu parades" formed behind Junior as he walked the streets of Brownsville. Roosevelt, who also ran on the Liberal Party's line, faced a formidable opponent: Congressman Jacob Javits, a liberal Republican who represented Upper Manhattan. The Republicans also fielded a similarly liberal candidate for governor, then U.S. senator Irving Ives (from tiny Chenango County in the Catskills). Unlike Ives, Javits had a strong relationship with unions. When the dust settled, Harriman defeated Ives by a whisker, while Javits convincingly triumphed over Roosevelt. Although both Democrats easily carried Brooklyn, Harriman collected over 50,000 more votes than Junior. The Sanders family's district, however, turned out nearly identical large margins for both Harriman and Roosevelt, thus illustrating Eleanor's enduring clout in the area. For her part, Roosevelt blamed her son's loss on Tammany boss Carmine de Sapio, causing the former First Lady to initiate a protracted behind-the-scenes campaign that brought about Tammany's eventual demise in 1961.[202]

With Wagner at City Hall and now Harriman in the Governor's Mansion in Albany, the New Deal was firmly back in place in New York. But even without full-throttled support, FDR's twin-engine machine—combining public works and large social spending—had never really

202   *Brooklyn Eagle* (10-4-1954) and *New York Times* (10-4-1954).

been sidelined. In May 1954, the *Brooklyn Eagle* published a map that showed how over $1 billion in public money was being spent on projects across the borough. Robert Moses had commandeered $60 million for the Brooklyn-Queens Expressway and Prospect Expressway, and the same amount was allocated to subway expansions, including an aerial stretch of the Culver Line in Gowanus (now F and G trains) and a planned extension of the Nostrand Avenue Line (now the 2 and 5). From Coney Island to Bushwick, nearly $400 million was being spent on more than two dozen public housing projects. Another $40 million was earmarked for health centers, including nearly $18 million for new buildings at Coney Island Hospital. And more than $5 million was being spent on new or renovated libraries. [203]

Along with their Midwood neighbors, Larry and Bernie most directly benefited from the new Kings Highway Branch of the Brooklyn Public Library that opened with great fanfare in October 1954. As Larry recalls, prior to that, the branch was in makeshift locations, including the second floor of a local firehouse with a narrow stairwell. Now the residents of Midwood had a state-of-the-art $800,000 library of their own. Although Larry says Bernie was not an avid reader through his high school years, the brothers made frequent use of their new

203 *Brooklyn Eagle* (5-23-1954).

local library in order for Larry to do his classwork from Brooklyn College and Bernie to do his homework from Madison High School. As Bernie told a Vermont paper in the early 1980s, "books and intellectual ideas were not topics of discussion with my parents." It was Larry, he said, who "introduced [him] to poetry and brought Freud and political ideas home with him" from Brooklyn College.[204] The family indeed kept only a few books in their small apartment but the shelf was an eclectic mix, including a collection of the writings of Spinoza, the seventeenth-century Portuguese-Jewish rationalist philosopher; Margaret Mead's 1936 novel *Gone with the Wind*, which had sold millions of copies and become a fixture in American living rooms; and a book of human anatomy full of diagrams. There was no question which of the three was most popular with the Sanders boys and their friends. As with many of their neighbors, it was the *New York Post* that furnished a constant stream of new reading material for the Sanders family. "Every Brooklyn Jewish household read it," says Bernie's high school classmate Myron Kalin.

Although he's largely forgotten today, the *Post*'s leading figure throughout the 1950s was Max Lerner, a household name during the era. Like James Wechsler, the paper's editor, Lerner was a former leftist turned Cold War liberal (and

204   Jaffe, 29.

strong supporter of Israel), but also a critic of McCarthy's witch hunts. Unlike Wechsler, Lerner's syndicated columns spanned well beyond politics. He helped popularize Alfred Kinsey's ground-breaking studies of sexual behavior (giving Lerner a reputation as an early advocate of gay equality), delivered psychologists' interpretations of pressing social problems like juvenile delinquency, and interpreted the meaning of murder cases, Broadway plays, and TV game shows. Amidst the Rosenberg case, Lerner attended a meeting of the couple's supporters held in Flatbush in June 1952. As he told *Post* readers, his sympathies lay with the attendees, "almost all of them Jewish residents of Brooklyn," who were unaware that the "Communist clique" who ran the meeting ultimately cared little about the Rosenbergs' fate. Reporting from Sing Sing in the wake of the execution one year later, Lerner—despite his contempt for the duo of "Communist fanatic[s]"—viewed the punishment as ultimately a public relations victory for the Kremlin. That fall, Lerner served up a three-column presentation of Freud to his readers, assuring them that the great psychoanalyst "had to wrestle with his demons. And out of that wrestling, one can surmise, came a measure of his strength and final assurance."[205] Such decidedly

---

205   After the success of his 1957 book *America as a Civilization*, Lerner
      compiled his *Post* columns from the period in *The Unfinished Country:
      A Book of Symbols* (New York: Simon and Schuster, 1959). Rosenberg
      columns on 483–490 and Freud series on 649–657. Born in Minsk,

middlebrow analysis earned Lerner the scorn of the era's highbrow critics.[206] But the protean columnist's signature mix of humanism, pluralism, and curiosity regarding both high and low culture helped shape the sensibility of his large audiences in Brooklyn and elsewhere.

The *Post* lent its support to Adlai Stevenson's second run against Ike in 1956, highlighting the candidate's late October visit to the Bronx on its front page. According to the caption beneath a half-page photo of Adlai waving to supporters, the crowd of 15,000 on the Grand Concourse was the largest ever in the Bronx for a political candidate.[207] *Post* columnist Murray Kempton, then in his late thirties, was considered to be one of Adlai's most ardent proponents. After her continued advocacy for Stevenson caused a rift with the *World-Telegram's* publisher, Eleanor Roosevelt joined Kempton and Lerner at the *Post*. Although support for Adlai remained strong in the Sanders family's

Russia, Lerner (1902–1997) moved to the U.S. at an early age and grew up in Bayonne, New Jersey, and later New Haven, Connecticut.

206   In March 1960, Midge Decter reviewed *The Unfinished Country* in *Commentary*, the leading outlet for conservative Jewish intellectuals during the period. Decter dismissively noted that "Lerner gently but earnestly lectures, prods, explains, always acting as the middleman and message-bearer between the professional students of American civilization—primarily the sociologists and social psychologists—and their subjects. But he is less a popularizer than a counsellor." Decter is the longtime spouse of the magazine's figurehead, Norman Podhoretz, who was born (in 1930) and raised in Brownsville.

207   *New York Post* (10-25-1956).

district, which went nearly 75 percent for the Democrat, Stevenson won Brooklyn by only 100,000 votes. In repeating his landslide victory, Ike now carried New York State with 61 percent. Perhaps most ominous was the decline in turnout in Brooklyn, which saw a drop-off of over 110,000 votes from 1952 to 1956. The vast majority of those were Democrats, many of whom had joined the flight of the borough's ethnic working class to Long Island's Nassau County. Brooklyn's postwar heyday was short-lived, and by the mid-1950s its political influence had begun to taper off.[208]

208   Vote totals in *New York Times* (11-5-1952 and 11-7-1956).

CHAPTER TEN: TRACK STAR

Bernie Sanders attended James Madison High School from the fall of 1955 through the spring of 1959. He joined a student body with clear, albeit uneven, expectations for the future. Unlike in present-day New York City, ninth-graders at that time enrolled in the high school closest to their homes. As Bernie's classmate Lou Howort recalls, this meant that among the 1,500–1,600 students at Madison there were two main groups of students: upper-middle-class kids from single-family homes and working- and lower-middle-class renters like Bernie. While the elite group expected to attend Ivy League and other top private colleges, their less well-off classmates saw CUNY on their horizon (and others embarked on vocational careers). The college-bound culture of the school was reflected in the pages of Madison's newspaper, the *Highway* (the name itself evoking people "on the move"). In addition to front-page stories about the school's Honor Society and its National Merit Scholarship finalists, the paper's first edition in Bernie's senior year ran a story about recent

Madison alums doing well at Harvard, Columbia, Barnard, and other elite institutions. Demographically, the school was almost entirely white—or over 75 percent Jewish, over 20 percent Italian and Irish, and the remainder black. According to Myron Kalin and Steve Slavin, the school's prevailing liberal integrationist sensibility was illustrated by the fact that a black student named James Dyer was voted school president during one of the years Bernie attended Madison.[209]

Bernie was a star athlete at Madison. He had been playing basketball since elementary school—and recent footage of him on the presidential campaign trail illustrates that he has carried with him a textbook set-shot technique. But he didn't make the varsity squad at Madison, and it was instead on the track where he excelled. By his sophomore year, he had become what a later Madison yearbook called a "standout" runner. In May 1957, the Madison team competed in the Public School Athletic League's Brooklyn track and field championship at Red Hook Stadium (now the ball fields), just a few blocks from Keystone Paints. There Bernie finished third in the one-mile run, which earned him his first appearance in the *New York Times*. In his junior year, Bernie became co-captain of the track team and over the

---

209 *Madison Highway* (10-8-1958). Myron Kalin's father owned a laundromat, and Lou Howort's father was a property manager at Trump Village in Coney Island.

next two years his efforts garnered several mentions and photos in the *Highway*. In the fall 1958 PSAL championships (held at Van Cortlandt Park in the Bronx), Bernie and Lou Howort finished third and fourth in the Brooklynwide two-and-a-half-mile run. As the *Times* again recorded, Bernie's 14:16 time placed him seven seconds behind the winner, Clarence Scott of Automotive High School on Bedford Avenue in Williamsburg. Scott's twin brother Joe finished second. At the citywide championships on November 7, 1958, the identical African American siblings were so far ahead of the pack that they held hands at the finish line, forcing the judges to choose Joe as the winner (Bernie came in eighteenth). A few days later, Bernie and Howort led Madison's cross-country team, known as the Krinskymen, to a boroughwide title.[210]

By his senior year at Madison, Bernie had begun to show a distinct interest in politics. When he was president of the Young Democrats at Brooklyn College, Larry had brought his younger brother to a few meetings, introducing him to issues and political organizing. But Bernie hadn't fully immersed himself in it. As Larry recalls, he and his parents thus were "all caught off-guard" when Bernie informed them in the fall of 1958 that he had entered

210 Philip Bump, "The Untold Story of Bernie Sanders, High School Track Star," *Washington Post* (1-29-2016); New York Times (5-22-1957, 10-31-1958 and 11-8-1958); and *Madison Highway* (11-20-1958).

the race for school president for the spring semester. In
the campaign Bernie was unafraid to take on issues that
were not obvious vote winners. Earlier in the fall, Myron
Kalin—who had been elected as treasurer of the student
government and would be named "most popular boy" in
the Madison senior yearbook—had helped spread word
about the plight of Korean War orphans. Kalin remembers first learning of the hardships faced by the 200,000
children in need (most of whom had been fathered by U.S.
soldiers) at a city government event for high school student leaders. Bernie, one of three candidates for school
president, made their plight central to his platform. "It was
so far out in terms of what we usually heard," Lou Howort
says, "that it went over students' heads—and I knew he
wouldn't get elected." Bernie indeed finished third. The
winner, Robert Rockfeld, had been the leader of Sing, the
school's very popular musical production group.[211] Bernie,
however, continued to serve as a fundraiser for Madison's
orphan support efforts, which included sponsoring an
elementary school student in Korea. With Rockfeld's
assistance, Bernie fulfilled a campaign pledge by organizing a charity basketball game in late March 1959.[212] In his

---

211   During Bernie's years at Madison, future 1970s pop star Carole King
      (b. 1942) participated in Sing productions.

212   For the charity game, which pitted the school's alumni versus the current
      varsity squad, Bernie hoped to recruit then New York Knicks coach Fuzzy
      Levane (1920-1912), a Madison graduate. *Madison Highway* (3-25-1959).

debut in political work, Bernie thus entered the arena as a humanitarian liberal.[213]

There were multiple distinct influences that shaped Bernie's emerging political sensibility. The Roosevelt legacy, which combined both FDR's New Deal blueprint with Eleanor's ongoing UN work, quite clearly made its mark. The cerebral Adlai Stevenson inspired many of his Democratic followers to support informed discussion of world affairs. Larry certainly provided a role model, given his political engagement while at Brooklyn College. Meanwhile, the callousness of unbridled capitalism was painted in stark terms by a development that affected something very close to the hearts of Bernie and many of his peers. By the summer of 1957, it was clear that Walter O'Malley was taking the Dodgers away from Brooklyn.

The move seemed to happen suddenly. In the fall of Bernie's freshman year, the "Bums" (as they were affectionately known) had finally knocked off the Yankees and won the World Series. Yet soon after his junior year began, they had played their final game at Ebbets Field. After losing four times to the Bronx Bombers since Jackie Robinson joined the club in 1947, the Dodgers' victory in the seventh game of the 1955 series caused the borough

213   Over his own photo in Myron Kalin's copy of the school yearbook, Bernie wrote, "Out of all the things I've ever done in Madison, working with you on the Korean Orphan program has been the most gratifying. Lots of love, Bernie."

to erupt in celebration. "Brooklyn's long cherished dream has finally come true," began the lead story on the front page of the *New York Times*, which featured a large photo of Roy Campanella holding pitcher Johnny Podres, the series hero, high in the air. "Far into the Flatbush night rang shouts of revelry," veteran *Times* sportswriter John Debinger noted at the end of his lengthy recap. Ominously, Debinger then declared that "Brooklyn has at long last won a world series and now let someone suggest moving the Dodgers elsewhere!"[214] At least one notable figure from Brooklyn's literary set got swept up in the fever, too. Poet Marianne Moore, who had lived on Cumberland Street in Fort Greene for over three decades, penned a tribute to the champions a year later. There was "pandemonium!" when Campanella "le[apt] high" after the last out, Moore wrote in the opening stanza. After at least one stanza featuring each of the team's key players, she then exhorted:

You've got plenty: Jackie Robinson
and Campy and Big Newk and Dodgerdom again
watching everything you do. You won last year.

Come on.[215]

---

214   *New York Times* (10-5-1955). *The Brooklyn Eagle* shut down in January 1955, leaving Brooklyn without a boroughwide publication.

215   Moore's poem was set to the tune of "Mama Gonna Buy You a Mockingbird."

Moore and her fellow Dodgers faithful nearly got their wish, as the team went to the 1956 series, only to fall in seven games to the Yankees. But their days in Brooklyn were numbered.

"Teams Set to Go Unless City Acts," warned the *New York Post*'s cover headline in late May 1957, in the wake of the permission the Dodgers and New York Giants received from league owners to move to the West Coast. Dodgers owner Walter O'Malley had persuaded his counterpart Horace Stoneham to bring his club to San Francisco. Though they had won the World Series in 1954 and featured great black players including Willie Mays, the Giants lacked a clear regional identity—and thus did not break as many hearts when they left town. "Hope Is Fading," read another headline on the front page of the *Post*'s sports section a few days later. As the paper reported, Mayor Wagner and other city officials declined to offer subsidies to the ball clubs in order to keep them from moving. Milton Gross, one of the *Post*'s two main sports columnists, announced that the rapacious O'Malley was demanding the Chavez Ravine site in Downtown L.A. as an "outright gift." Gross angrily opined that the owner had "alienated" the team's Brooklyn fans, who "no longer care whether [the Dodgers] go or stay." Indicative of his clout, the *Post*'s other main sports columnist Jimmy Cannon sat down with Mayor Wagner for an hour at City Hall to discuss the issue.

Wagner, Cannon wrote, should not be the "fall guy." In his view, O'Malley and Stoneham were making the move for one main reason: large television contracts in fast-growing California markets.[216]

There were other legitimate business concerns for O'Malley, including the Dodgers' declining attendance at Ebbets Field and the lack of parking in the area for the many fans who had moved from the borough to Long Island. O'Malley had also been unsuccessful in his negotiations with the Wagner administration to build a new stadium at Flatbush and Atlantic in Downtown Brooklyn (now the location of the Barclays Center). Robert Moses was instead angling to bring the Dodgers to the site in Flushing Meadows, Queens, that he was eyeing as the future home of the 1964 World's Fair and what became Shea Stadium. Even as the league owners granted the two teams permission to move in May 1957, whether they would actually do so remained—at least officially—up in the air. O'Malley evaded questions from the *Post*'s Gross regarding whether the deal for the new Downtown Brooklyn site was still in negotiations. But the early-season actions of team's management helped make the move seem like a *fait accompli*, in the process driving down team attendance another 15

216   *New York Post* (5-29-1957 and 5-31-1957). Gross and Cannon were both staunch integrationists and allies of Jackie Robinson (who retired at the end of 1956). In the mid-1960s, Cannon—then writing in the *New York Journal-American*—became a bitter foe of Muhammad Ali.

percent in the Bums' final season at Ebbets Field. Although the 1957 squad featured mainstays including Campanella, Snider, and Hodges, in the Dodgers' final weekend at Ebbets Field, fewer than 7,000 fans showed up for each of the three games to say goodbye. Even before the season's end, the scars were intact.[217]

For Bernie's generation of Brooklynites, those wounds were permanent. The Dodgers leaving town served as a parable about loyalty, loss, and the decline of Brooklyn's identity as a thriving "major-league" place. By exposing the national pastime as just another business organized first and foremost around the pursuit of profit, O'Malley also taught Brooklyn youth a lesson about the nature of capitalism. It is a system in which, as Marx famously observed, "all that is holy is profaned." As Bernie told the *New York Times* on the 2020 campaign trail, "It was like they would move the Brooklyn Bridge to California." Although the upheaval was by no means the "sole reason" he became a democratic socialist, Bernie explained that "I did [find out] in that case about the greed of one particular company. And that impacted me." He waxed nostalgic about going to games at Ebbets Field, where bleacher seats cost sixty cents. Bernie's Madison pal Myron Kalin says the kids in their

217 In *Brooklyn: The Once and Future City* (2019), historian Thomas Campanella argues, "Ultimately, what propelled the Dodgers out of town was neither O'Malley's duplicity nor Moses's stubbornness, but the loss of their fans" (446).

neighborhood used to ride their bicycles past Gil Hodges' house on Bedford Avenue (only two blocks from the Sanders family's apartment). The Dodgers of the Jackie Robinson era "made us proud to proclaim we were from Brooklyn," recalls leading New York City civil rights attorney Norman Siegel, who was born in 1942 and raised in Borough Park. The "void" left by the team's move lingers to this day, says Siegel, who served as a longtime board member of the Jackie Robinson Foundation. Brooklyn College journalism professor Ron Howell—the grandson of Bertrand Baker, the borough's first black elected official— was eight in 1957 and lived in Bed-Stuy. Howell was the bat boy for the East Brooklyn Tigers, his nine-year-old cousin's little league team. Together they marched with other little leaguers, black and white, to Ebbets Field to protest the Dodgers' move. Like many of his peers, Bernie has indeed spent a lifetime fighting the Walter O'Malleys of the world.[218]

An even greater personal tragedy for the Sanders family began to unfold during Bernie's final years at Madison.

218 *New York Times* (1-30-2020). Siegel and Howell to author (January 2020). At the end of *The Boys of Summer*, his landmark 1972 work about the Brooklyn Dodgers, the late sportswriter Roger Kahn (1927–2020, raised in Prospect Heights) cemented O'Malley's reputation as a heartless, greedy businessman. During an interview in the early 1970s, O'Malley told the writer he was worth $24 million, at which point the owner "turned and gazed at his California stadium with delight." Two pages later, O'Malley's business partner Buzzy Bavasi informed Kahn that "All Walter left out were three hundred acres of downtown Los Angeles." Roger Kahn, *The Boys of Summer* (New York: Harper Perennial, 2006 ed.), 430–432.

His mother fell into a downward spiral. A bout with rheumatic fever in her youth had resulted in Dora's chronic heart problems, which now brought her in and out of the hospital. Medical bills became a problem for Eli. And as Bernie explained in his 1997 memoir, when it came time for Bernie to decide what he would do after high school, his parents had differing views. Eli, the struggling paint salesman, wanted Bernie to go find a steady job; Dora, the high school graduate—and daughter of an ardent Yiddish Socialist—urged Bernie to follow in his brother's footsteps and attend college.[219] Steve Slavin, who had run track with Bernie and was already attending Brooklyn College, explains that Bernie had been accepted to the University of Chicago while a senior at Madison but deferred for a year because of his mother's health. "Not many of our peers would have done that," says Slavin. Bernie thus entered Brooklyn College—which had free tuition—in the fall of 1959. The following March, after a second heart surgery failed, Dora Sanders passed away at the very young age of forty-six. Larry, who had returned from Harvard Law to help care for his mother, stuck around to help his father, who was now "desperately depressed."[220]

Bernie thus spent only one academic year at Brooklyn College. As Steve Slavin explains, because of strained

219 Sanders, *Outsider in the House*, 14.

220 Kelley, "Bernie's Bro."

relations with his father, Bernie moved out of the family apartment on E. 26th Street. He and Slavin shared the attic apartment of a large Victorian house on 798 E. 21st Street, two blocks from Brooklyn College. The homeowner was a Madison High School Latin teacher, and Slavin recalls that she was "very unpleasant." The two friends split a large room, each paying $40 per month. Steve says he assumed Bernie had saved money from working as a camp counselor at Ten Mile River; during the holiday season, Bernie also worked as a temporary mail carrier for the Post Office. Freshmen at Brooklyn College took various introductory courses, including a required four-credit English class. According to Russell Banks, who profiled the then-mayor of Burlington in 1985, Bernie's "one major political act during his year-long stay at Brooklyn College was to write a letter to the editor of the school newspaper complaining about regulation against sitting on the campus grass."[221]

Slavin recalls that rather than coursework or campus politics, Bernie was more engaged by the reading material he found in the library. At final exam time, students were allowed to check out unlimited numbers of books, and Steve says Bernie came home with as many as he could carry. One that Bernie particularly enjoyed was a biography of John Peter Altgeld, who was governor of Illinois in

---

221   Russell Banks, "Bernie Sanders, the Socialist Mayor," *The Atlantic* (10-5-2015).

the mid-1890s. During the Pullman Strike—led by Eugene Debs[222]—that shut down the national railroads in 1894, Altgeld tried to block President Grover Cleveland from sending federal troops into his state. Though both he and Cleveland were Democrats, Altgeld was an ally of the president's main rival in the party, populist William Jennings Bryan. In a preview of his recent political career, Bernie thus began to identify with the left-wing of the Democrats. And after he arrived at the University of Chicago for the fall semester of 1960, his reverence for Debs and socialism fully flowered.[223]

Like many of his peers at Brooklyn College, Bernie was restless. In a December 1958 *Harper's* profile of the CUNY institution, Brooklyn College English professor David Boroff noted that many of the 15,000 students on campus had "a sense of marginality" because they "had been denied that special badge of status—the out-of-town school." "We're imitation Ivy League," one student explained to Boroff.[224]

---

222 As Bernie told Russell Banks, he initially became familiar with Debs on his first day at Brooklyn College. At an orientation event, he came across the table for the campus Eugene V. Debs Club. when he asked why they were named after Debs, a fellow student told him, "We're the local socialists." Bernie informed Banks that he was "amazed" because "Here were real live socialists sitting right in front of me!"

223 Jason Horowitz, "Bernie Sanders's '100% Brooklyn' Roots Are as Unshakeable as His Accent," *New York Times* (7-27-2015).

224 David Boroff, "Brooklyn College: Culture in Flatbush," *Harper's* (December 1958), 44.

Though it had been a hotbed of political activism in the 1930s (leading to its nickname as the "Little Red School House"),[225] by the late 1950s Brooklyn College was relatively quiet politically. That said, the college's faculty included the pioneering black historian John Hope Franklin. And the institution was duly recognized by elite colleges, as evidenced by Larry's acceptance at Harvard Law. Yet after his mother died, Bernie left Brooklyn, seeking a change of scenery along with that "special badge of status." Though it was declining in both national influence and population, the Brooklyn he departed would remain a Democratic stronghold. In many places across the nation, as well as in upstate New York, John F. Kennedy's Catholic identity sparked nativist resentment. But that was certainly not the case in Brooklyn, where the borough's Irish and Italian voters now united with the Jewish and black Roosevelt coalition. In November 1960, JFK won New York State by only 50,000 votes, making his nearly 2–1 margin (and 320,000 greater tallies) in Brooklyn essential to his victory. And in the Sanders family's district, JFK took home more than three-quarters of the vote.

---

225 The term was mentioned by the distinguished *New Yorker* writer John McPhee in his tour (the centerpiece of his 1982 work *In Suspect Terrain*) of Brooklyn with leading geologist Anita G. Harris, who was born in 1937, grew up in Williamsburg and attended Brooklyn College in the mid-1950s. As McPhee wrote, "Ebbets Field, where they buried the old Brooklyn Dodgers, was also on the terminal moraine. When a long-ball hitter hit a long ball, it would land on Bedford Avenue and bounce down the morainal front to roll toward Coney on the outwash plain. No one in Los Angeles would ever hit a homer like that."

CONCLUSION

It was on the South Side of Chicago where Bernie Sanders came of age politically. His leftward migration was somewhat ironic at the time, because Bernie had transferred from the "Little Red Schoolhouse" to an elite private institution, which he paid for via grants and student loans, and by working part-time jobs. "When I went to the University of Chicago," Bernie explained to a *Los Angeles Times* reporter in 1991, "I began to understand the futility of liberalism."[226] One of the political groups he joined was the Young People's Socialist League, an outgrowth of the Eugene Debs-era Socialist Party. (One of the group's national leaders, Tom Kahn, had attended Brooklyn College in the mid-1950s.)[227] In a 2016 interview aired on

---

226   Quoted in Carol Felsenthal, "Bernie Sanders Found Socialism at the University of Chicago," *Chicago* magazine (5-4-2015).

227   Kahn (1938–1992) attended Erasmus Hall High School in Flatbush, then Brooklyn College, before transferring to Howard University (as a white student). Openly gay, he became lovers with Socialist figurehead Bayard Rustin.

C-Span, Bernie shed light on why he joined the YPSL. "Ever
since I was a little kid, I really did not like to see bullies,"
he recalled, adding that "I felt strongly about racism, and
about poverty." As Bernie noted, the Socialists' critique
connected various forms of discrimination and exploita-
tion to war, linking all to the common driving force of capitalism.[228] As biographer Harry Jaffe observed regarding
the atmosphere in Hyde Park, "The socialist politics that
surrounded [Bernie] in Brooklyn prepared him for the university's radical milieu."[229] Bernie joined campus chapters
of the Student Peace Union, Congress of Racial Equality
(CORE), and the Student Non-Violent Coordinating
Committee. As chair of the CORE chapter's social action
committee,[230] he famously helped lead a 1962 sit-in protest
against the university's racially segregated campus housing policy. Like many of his peers, Bernie realized that the
cautious liberalism of the Democrats under Stevenson and
now Kennedy was an insufficient approach to rectify ine-
qualities of any kind.

In addition to his activism, Bernie first became fully
involved in electoral politics in Mayor Daley's Chicago.

---

228   Posting is dated C-Span (11-21-2016). See https://www.youtube.com/
      watch?v=j8-qOW78jYY.

229   Jaffe, 39.

230   Title Mentioned in Rick Perlstein, "A Political Education," *University of
      Chicago Magazine* (Jan/Feb 2015).

Long rumored to have been an active anti-black assailant in Chicago's race riot of 1919, Daley had controlled City Hall since 1955 and would not surrender it until his death in 1976. "Boss Daley" exerted influence over the large African American population on Chicago's South Side via what was known as his "sub-machine," a network of six black aldermen. A liberal enclave, Hyde Park's alderman was Leon Despres, an outspoken white critic of Daley known as the "lone Negro on the city council,"[231] his skin color notwithstanding. In 1963, Bernie worked on Despres's reelection campaign, which the Daley machine unsuccessfully tried to thwart. Illustrative of his principles, Despres had supported the CORE protest against the university's housing policy, placing the alderman in opposition to the largest institution in his district. While working on the campaign, "I was very impressed by Richard J. Daley's Chicago machine," Sanders told historian Rick Perlstein, with a note of sarcasm. The Tammany-style patronage operation, Bernie recalled, had "a city worker for every two hundred votes." Yet as Bernie had also seen in his hometown, the Democratic Party was often an obstacle to social justice.

As Perlstein detailed, the campus CORE protest occurred amid the larger backlash against urban renewal witnessed in New York City, Chicago, and many other cities.

In 1961, a *Harper's* excerpt from Jane Jacobs's *Death and Life of American Cities* ended by spotlighting large urban planning initiatives near the campus that had been supported by the University of Chicago. The results had further segregated white Hyde Park from its black South Side neighbors. At the same time in New York City, Larry Sanders became active with the Bolivar-Douglass Club, a reform organization (i.e., opponent of the Democratic Party machine) on the Lower East Side. Larry recalls helping the club protest the proposed Tompkins Square Housing Site plan put forth by Robert Moses and the Wagner administration. Aligned with Jane Jacobs, white activists joined with the area's large Puerto Rican community in an unsuccessful effort to make the project address the needs of lower-income residents.[232] By mid-decade, America's segregated cities had become ticking time bombs.

The Sanders brothers' Yiddish Socialism continued to steer their political activism. After Bernie graduated in 1964, both he and Larry went to Israel to spend time on separate kibbutzim. Bernie spent six months at a Marxist kibbutz in northern Israel. According to a 2015 profile in *Tablet*, Larry stayed in Israel until 1967.[233] Larry says

---

232   For details of Tompkins Square organizing, see Arthur R. Simon, "New Yorkers without a Voice: The Tragedy of Urban Renewal," *The Atlantic* (April 1966).

233   Jas Chana, "Straight Out of Brooklyn, by Way of Vermont," *Tablet* (8-20-2015). During his first run, the liberal Israeli paper *Haaretz*

that when he returned to the U.S. that year, he stayed at Bernie's apartment that was also near Brooklyn College. The Sanders brothers were now on their own. In August 1962, Eli Sanders died, only fifty-seven years old. After returning from Israel, Bernie—and his first wife, Deborah Shiling (m. 1964–1966), whom he met at the University of Chicago—bought property in Vermont. For the next few years, Bernie bounced back and forth between there, Brooklyn, and Manhattan, where he and his friends started a business called Creative Carpentry that advertised in the *Village Voice*.[234] While in Brooklyn, Bernie taught in the Head Start program that was a prominent Great Society initiative of LBJ's administration. During the same period, he applied for Conscientious Objector status in order not to go to Viet Nam. Jews were not recognized as a group that opposed war on religious grounds, but the proceedings in Bernie's case extended beyond the time period in which he was eligible to be drafted. In 1968, he moved to Vermont full-time and Larry soon called England home.

The Brooklyn in which his current wife, Jane O'Meara (b. 1950), grew up and attended high school was a far more

reported (on 2-4-2016) that Bernie told an interviewer in 1990 that he went to Kibbutz Sha'ar Ha'amakim as part of the Hashomer Hatzair youth movement. According to a follow-up *Haaretz* story (2-9-2016), the kibbutz was a stronghold of socialism, and it was affiliated with Israel's leftist party Mapam that had supported Stalin.

234 Margaret Talbot, "The Populist Prophet," *The New Yorker* (10-12-2015).

divided place than what Bernie knew only a decade earlier. By the mid-1960s vast swathes of Central Brooklyn
had become a mostly black ghetto. The former Jewish
stronghold of Brownsville was now a dilapidated black
and Puerto Rican slum. It was also the site of the landmark
teachers strike of 1968 that pit Albert Shanker's largely
Jewish union versus neighborhood activists seeking community control over schools (which included the right
to hire black and Puerto Rican teachers).[235] Firebrands
like CORE's Sonny Carson and those affiliated with the
Brooklyn chapter of the Black Panther Party clashed with
the race-baiting Shanker. The resulting split between
Brooklyn's Jewish liberals and its post-civil rights black
leadership would help fuel the rise of Mayor Ed Koch a
decade later. In the section of East Flatbush where O'Meara
lived, and in the area surrounding Park Slope (where she
attended St. Saviour High School), racial animosity flour-
ished among white ethnics. In "The Revolt of the White
Lower Middle Class," a 1969 feature story in *New York* magazine, Park Slope's own Pete Hamill (b. 1935)[236] memorably depicted the cauldron of hostilities flowing from the
bar stools at Farrell's and other watering holes in Windsor

---

235 For overview, see Mike Stivers, "Ocean Hill-Brownsville, 50 Years Later,"
     Jacobin (September 2018).

236 Hamill got his start at the *New York Post* after writing a letter to James
     Wechsler in 1960. *New York Times* (1-10-1994).

Terrace. The Irish and Italian hard hats there hated Mayor John Lindsay (1966–1973), a liberal Republican with close ties to the city's minority communities. "The niggers get the schools...the niggers get the new playgrounds...And they get it all without workin'," ranted one ironworker.[237] A few months later, Hamill's pal Jimmy Breslin—who had briefly run for mayor that year, on a ticket with Norman Mailer—rode through Park Slope with Lindsay. Breslin described the Puerto Rican area along 5th Avenue near Atlantic and Flatbush as "hot and ramshackle and dirty and crowded ... their visible surroundings seem so hopeless."[238] Ascendant in the era of Jackie Robinson and Woody Guthrie, by the end of the 1960s racial hostility and turf wars were now the prevailing terrain of Brooklyn.

Brooklyn's large reservoir of Democratic voters none-theless remained influential. Wielding his clout from Canarsie, party boss Meade Esposito helped propel inef-fectual party insider Abe Beame to victory in the mayoral election of 1973 and then played a pivotal role in Koch's triumph four years later. In 1974, Park Slope congressman Hugh Carey prevailed in the race for governor. None of these figures was a committed New Dealer. In dealing with

---

237   Pete Hamill, "The Revolt of the White Lower Middle Class," *New York* (4-14-1969).

238   Jimmy Breslin, "Is Lindsay Too Tall to be Mayor?" *New York* (7-28-1969). Breslin (1928–2017) grew up in Queens and attended John Adams High School in Ozone Park.

the fiscal crisis, Beame agreed to impose tuition at CUNY, raise subway fares, and rein in public sector spending. Carey at the same time helped create the New York State Financial Control Board, which ensures that the city will not run deficits (thus undermining its ability to fund public works projects). Koch ran in 1977 as a law-and-order Democrat who pitched his campaign to outer-borough white ethnics while attacking public-sector unions. In office, he catered to Midtown developers led by Donald Trump and rolled back city spending on health care and other social services. Even with a Democrat in the White House in the late 1970s, the New Deal was visibly in decline in the city where it originated.[239]

The cultural landscape also shifted considerably in Brooklyn from the late 1940s through the mid-1970s. After the Dodgers left, the borough lacked not only a professional sports team[240] but also any comparable symbol of interracial, multi-ethnic unity. Jackie Robinson nonetheless remained a prominent figure in the borough until his death in 1972. As a columnist in the *Amsterdam News*, Robinson, formerly a liberal Republican, moved to the

---

239   For further details on the politics of the fiscal crisis era, see Freeman, *Working-Class New York*; and Phillips-Fein, *Fear City*.

240   Even without the Dodgers, Brooklyn still played a significant marketing role for Major League Baseball (and several other professional sports). Through the early 1990s, the headquarters of Topps trading cards was at Bush Terminal on the Sunset Park waterfront.

left throughout the decade. In September 1968, upwards of 150 white NYPD officers—many of whom supported segregationist presidential candidate George Wallace— attacked members of the Black Panther Party at the Brooklyn courthouse.[241] Incensed, Robinson spoke out in defense of the Panthers and called on Mayor Lindsay to take action against the officers.[242] Before he died, Robinson also expressed regret for his HUAC testimony regarding Paul Robeson, stating that "if asked now," he would reject the invitation. Robeson, he observed, had "sacrificed himself, his career, and the wealth and comfort he once enjoyed because, I believe, he was sincerely trying to help his people."[243] In the last years of his life, Jackie and Rachel Robinson's circle of friends included Howard Cosell (1918–1995), the prominent sportscaster who grew up in Sheepshead Bay. Throughout the 1960s, Cosell was a leading ally of Muhammad Ali. Although Brooklyn had been formative in both of their careers, Cosell, who lived

---

241   For details, see Jarrod Shanahan, "'White Tigers Eat Black Panthers': New York City's Law Enforcement Group," Gotham Center for New York History blog (3-21-2019).

242   "The conduct of the Black Panthers has been admirable," Robinson wrote in the *Amsterdam News* (9-21-1968) following the courthouse violence. That same issue featured a photo of Jackie clasping hands with the Brooklyn Panthers' leadership.

243   Peter Dreier, "Half a Century Before Colin Kaepernick, Jackie Robinson Said, 'I Cannot Stand and Sing the National Anthem," *The Nation* (7-18-2019).

in an affluent area of Westchester County, New York, now visited the Robinsons in Stamford, Connecticut.[244] Arthur Miller lived in Roxbury, Connecticut, fifty miles away.

Like Jackie Robinson, Woody Guthrie died in his mid-fifties. Although he spent most of the first half of the 1960s in Brooklyn, Guthrie's Huntington's Disease had taken its toll. From 1961–1966, he was in a mental institution then called Brooklyn State Hospital (now Kingsboro Psychiatric Center) in East Flatbush. After moving to Creedmoor Psychiatric Center in Queens Village, Woody passed away in early October 1967, just as his son Arlo's career began to take off. The year before Arlo was born, Woody penned "Go Coney Island, Roll on the Sand" (1946), a playful song about his Mermaid Avenue surroundings, with the chorus repeating its title. After Woody was cremated at Brooklyn's Green-Wood Cemetery, his ashes were given to his children Arlo and Nora, who headed down to Coney. After prying open the canister, Arlo heaved it toward the water, with Guthrie's ashes rolling across the sand.[245] While mayor of Burlington two decades later, Bernie would record a version of "This Land Is Your Land," and in the 2016 campaign, he led audiences in sing-alongs

244   Rampersad, 313 and 432.

245   Cray, 391–392.

of it at his rallies. In February 2020, Arlo joined Bernie on the trail in North Carolina.

The ghost of Willy Loman has lingered throughout Bernie's political career. After a relatively quiet first few years in the U.S. Senate, Sanders gained widespread notoriety in 2010 after his nearly nine-hour filibuster in opposition to the Obama administration's extension of Bush-era tax cuts for the rich. Two years later, after he cruised to reelection with just over 70 percent of the vote, the *New York Times* profiled the Vermont senator. "Bernard Sanders, Gruff Voice for Shielding Entitlements" read the original headline, previewing the paper of record's dismissive stance towards Sanders during his two presidential campaigns. Reporter Sheryl Gay Stolberg nonetheless provided an insightful portrayal. At the time, Sanders was leading the charge against the bipartisan initiative (supported by the Obama-Biden administration) to reduce the federal deficit by cutting Social Security, Medicaid, and Medicare. "After four years of accusing Mr. Obama of practicing 'European-style socialism,'" Goldberg noted, Sanders' Senate colleagues were "hardly enamored of a man who actually embraces European-style socialism, and who carries a brass key chain from the presidential campaign of Eugene V. Debs." Citing Sweden and Finland as his models, Bernie said he wanted the federal government to expand its entitlements to include health care and childcare. "His philosophy," Stolberg wrote, "flows from his Brooklyn boyhood home." "Money was always a source of friction," Bernie said, invoking Willy Loman. As the senator explained, Arthur Miller's greatest character offered a lesson that his colleagues needed to learn regarding "people who have money not understanding what it's like not to have money."[246]

On a cold Saturday afternoon in early March 2019, Bernie formally launched his 2020 campaign before 10,000 supporters on the quad of Brooklyn College. "I was born and raised a few miles from here in a three-and-a-half-room rent-controlled apartment," Bernie told the crowd. "My father was a paint salesman who worked hard his entire life but never made much money." Rent control, the handiwork of the American Labor Party (and a Republican governor), had enabled his family to stay in their home while Larry and Bernie got their education. As Bernie further noted, "My mother's dream was that someday our family would move out of that rent-controlled apartment to a home of our own. That dream was never fulfilled." His values had been shaped by economic struggle, Bernie said, contrasting himself with the silver spooner now occupying the White House, who grew up in

---

246 The headline now reads, "In Fiscal Debate, an Unvarnished Voice for Shielding Benefits," *New York Times* (12-14-2012). Rather than "entitlements" or "benefits," Sanders calls pensions, health care, etc. "rights."

Jamaica Estates, Queens. "I did not have a father who gave me millions of dollars to build luxury skyscrapers, casinos, and country clubs," he declared. On the campaign trail one year later, Bernie invoked the ghost of Walter O'Malley. He denounced a proposal by Major League Baseball that would end minor league farm teams, and thus undermine smaller cities like Burlington, where Bernie helped bring a franchise in the 1980s. At the end of a *New York Times* story about his childhood enthusiasm for the Dodgers and advocacy on behalf of minor league baseball, Bernie brought up an old joke. By the end of 1957, he quipped, the three most hated people in Brooklyn were Hitler, Stalin, and Walter O'Malley—"not necessarily in that order."

Had a poll been taken in the late 1950s of who were the most beloved figures in Brooklyn, FDR and Eleanor most certainly would have been at the top of the list. At the 2016 Democratic National Convention in Philadelphia, Larry Sanders provided a most poignant reminder of the Roosevelts' legacy. A member of Democrats Abroad, a group that casts delegate votes in the primary, Larry first invoked the names of Eli Sanders and Dorothy Glassberg Sanders. "They did not have easy lives, and they died young," an emotional Larry stated, as Bernie fought back tears. Eli and Dora "would be immensely proud of their son and his accomplishments," Larry continued, adding that "they loved the New Deal of Franklin Roosevelt—and they would be especially proud that Bernard is renewing that vision." Bernie and Jane O'Meara Sanders were visibly moved by the powerful tribute. But as the 2020 campaign unfolded, it was clear that in order to defeat the hatemonger from Queens, Bernie would first need to overcome powerful Democratic opposition to the New Deal in the city where it was launched. Brooklyn's two most prominent national leaders, Senator Chuck Schumer and Representative Hakeem Jeffries, are both staunch corporate-friendly neoliberals. In early 2019, Schumer, a Madison High School alum, joined with Nancy Pelosi and other party leaders in the "stop-Bernie" effort that hatched centrist Mayor Pete Buttigieg as a national contender.[247] In the 2016 campaign, Jeffries led the local attack for Hillary, dubbing Bernie a "gun-loving socialist with zero foreign policy experience." While Bernie's 2020 campaign has drawn support from progressive Mayor Bill de Blasio, a Brooklyn politician and quasi-New Dealer (who supported Hillary in 2016), de Blasio's predecessor spent unprecedented amounts of money against Sanders. Oligarch Mike Bloomberg quite cynically entered the race in order to thwart Bernie from implementing a modern New Deal. In his fight to restore the blueprint created by FDR, Bernie's political journey has thus come full circle.

---

247   Jonathan Martin, "'Stop Sanders' Democrats Are Agonizing over His Momentum," *New York Times* (4-16-2019).

Despite the formidable opposition to the New Deal, the global coronavirus pandemic and resulting economic crisis make a renewal of FDR's vision all the more urgent. FDR and Eleanor Roosevelt championed an activist role for the federal government in meeting the essential needs of the American people. They also advocated for international cooperation via the United Nations. Amid the public health emergency, Bernie has issued forceful calls for Medicare for All and for vast expansions in social spending. Throughout the 2020 campaign he has also frequently invoked the UN in his discussions of foreign policy. At the mid-March CNN debate with Joe Biden, Sanders touted the Green New Deal as a plan to address both the climate and economic crises. In both substance and style, Bernie continues to pay homage to the Roosevelt legacy. On the Saturday night prior to the CNN debate, Bernie delivered a fireside chat via his campaign website while sitting next to an active wood stove in his Burlington living room. Eli and Dora Sanders would be immensely proud, indeed.

BIBLIOGRAPHY

Badger, Emily. "How Redlining's Racist Effects Lasted for Decades," *New York Times* (8-24-2017).

Banks, Russell. "Bernie Sanders: The Once and Future Socialist." *The Atlantic* (10-5-2015).

Bayor, Ronald. *Neighbors in Conflict: The Irish, Germans, Jews and Italians of New York City, 1929–1941.* Baltimore: John Hopkins University Press, 1978.

Biondi, Martha. *To Stand and Fight: The Struggle for Civil Rights in Postwar New York City.* Cambridge, MA: Harvard University Press, 2006.

Bluestein, Gene. "Moses Asch, Documentor," *American Music* (Fall 1987).

Boroff, David. "Brooklyn College: Culture in Flatbush," *Harper's* (December 1958).

Breslin, Jimmy. "Is Lindsay Too Tall to be Mayor?" *New York* (7-28-1969).

Bump, Philip. "The Untold Story of Bernie Sanders, High School Track Star," *Washington Post* (1-29-2016).

Campanella, Thomas J. *Brooklyn: The Once and Future City.* Princeton, NJ: Princeton University Press, 2019.

Caro, Robert A. *The Power Broker: Robert Moses and the Fall of New York.* New York: Vintage, 1975.

Carpenter, Les. "How the Dodgers and Baseball Shaped Bernie Sanders' World View, *The Guardian* (10-27-2015).

Chana, Jas. "Straight Out of Brooklyn, by Way of Vermont," *Tablet* (8-20-2015).

Cook. Blanche Wisen. *Eleanor Roosevelt: The War Years and After.* New York: Penguin, 2016.

Cray, Ed. *Ramblin' Man: The Life and Times of Woody Guthrie.* New York: W.W. Norton, 2004.

Denning, Michael. *The Cultural Front: The Laboring of American Culture in the Twentieth Century.* New York: Verso, 1996.

Diaz, Danella. "Bernie Sanders: My Family Was Wiped Out by Hitler in the Holocaust," CNN.com (3-7-16).

Dreier, Peter. "Half a Century Before Colin Kaepernick, Jackie Robinson Said, 'I Cannot Stand and Sing the National Anthem," *The Nation* (7-18-2019).

Eig, Jonathan. *Opening Day: The Story of Jackie Robinson's First Season.* New York: Simon & Schuster, 2007.

Fay, William. "The Cities of America: Brooklyn," *Saturday Evening Post* (3-25-1950).

Felsenthal, Carol. "Bernie Sanders Found Socialism at the University of Chicago," *Chicago* (5-4-2015).

Freeman, Joshua B. *Working-Class New York: Life and Labor since World War II*. New York: New Press, 2000.

Greenfield, Jeff. "The Year the Veepstakes Really Mattered," *Politico Magazine* (July 2016).

Gunther, John. *Inside U.S.A.* New York: Harper & Brothers, 1947.

Guthrie, Nora. *My Name is New York: Ramblin' Around Woody Guthrie's Town*. Brooklyn, NY: powerHouse Books, 2014.

Hamill, Pete. "The Revolt of the White Lower Middle Class," *New York* (4-14-1969).

Haygood, Wil. *The King of the Cats: The Life and Times of Adam Clayton Powell, Jr.* New York: HarperCollins, 2006 ed.

Hoffman, Nicholas von. *Citizen Cohn: The Life and Times of Roy Cohn*. New York: Doubleday, 1988.

Horowitz, Jason. "Bernie Sanders's '100% Brooklyn' Roots Are as Unshakeable as His Accent," *New York Times* (7-27-2015).

Iling, Sean. "'We're Losing Our Damn Minds': James Carville Unloads on the Democratic Party," *Vox* (2-7-2020).

Jacobs, Jane. *The Death and Life of Great American Cities*. New York: Random House, 1961.

Jaffe, Harry. *Why Bernie Sanders Matters*. New York: Regan Arts, 2016.

Kahn, Roger. *The Boys of Summer*. New York: Harper Perennial, 2006 ed.

Katz, Daniel. "The Key to Bernie Sanders' Appeal Isn't Socialism. It's Yiddish Socialism," *The Forward* (2-14-2016).

Kaufman, Will. *Woody Guthrie: American Radical*. Urbana, IL: University of Illinois Press, 2011.

Kaufman, Will. "Woody Guthrie, 'Old Man Trump,' and a Real Estate Empire's Racist Foundations," *The Conversation* (1-21-2016).

Kaufman, Will. "In Another Newly Discovered Song, Woody Guthrie Continues His Assault on 'Old Man Trump,'" *The Conversation* (9-5-2016).

Kelley, Kevin. "Bernie's Bro: Bernie's Working-Class Brooklyn Roots Shaped My Brother," *Seven Days* (5-27-2015).

Klein, Joe. *Woody Guthrie: A Life*. New York: Random House, 1999 ed.

Leibovich, Mark. "The Socialist Senator," *New York Times Magazine* (1-21-2007).

Lerner, Max. *The Unfinished Country: A Book of Symbols*. New York: Simon and Schuster, 1959.

Martin, Jonathan. "'Stop Sanders' Democrats Are Agonizing over His Momentum," *New York Times* (4-16-2019).

McPhee, John. *In Suspect Terrain*. New York: Farrar, Straus and Giroux, 1982.

Meyer, Gerald. *Vito Marcantonio: Radical Politician, 1902-1954*. Albany, NY: SUNY Press, 1989.

Miller, Arthur. "A Boy Grew in Brooklyn," *Holiday* (March 1955).

Perlstein, Rick. "A Political Education," *University of Chicago Magazine* (Jan/Feb 2015).

Petrusich, Amanda. "A Story about Fred Trump and Woody Guthrie for the Midterm Elections," *New Yorker* (11-6-2018).

Phillips-Fein, Kim. *Fear City: New York's Fiscal Crisis and the Rise of Austerity Politics* (New York: Metropolitan Books, 2017).

Rampersad, Arnold. *Jackie Robinson: A Biography*. New York: Knopf, 1997.

Rothstein, Richard. *The Color of Law: How Our Government Segregated America*. New York: Liveright, 2017.

Sanders, Bernie, with Huck Gutman. *Outsider in the House*. New York: Verso Books, 1997.

Schneir, Walter and Schneir, Miriam. *Invitation to an Inquest: A New Look at the Rosenberg-Sobell Case*. New York: Doubleday, 1965.

Schwartz, Joel. "Tenant Power in the Liberal City, 1943-1971," in Ronald Lawson (with Mark Naison), ed., *The*

Tenant Movement in New York City, 1904-1984. New Brunswick, NJ: Rutgers University Press, 1986.

Shaw, Irwin. "Brooklyn," *Holiday* (June 1950).

Simon, Arthur R. "New Yorkers without a Voice: The Tragedy of Urban Renewal," *The Atlantic* (April 1966).

Stapinski, Helene. "Arthur Miller's Brooklyn," *New York Times* (1-24-2016).

Stolberg, Sheryl Gay. "In the Fiscal Debate, an Unvarnished Voice for Shielding Benefits," *New York Times* (12-13-2012).

Strausbaugh, John. *Victory City: A History of New York and New Yorkers During World War II.* New York: Twelve, 2018.

Sylvester, Robert. "Brooklyn Boy Makes Good," *Saturday Evening Post* (7-16-1949).

Talbot, Margaret. "The Populist Prophet," *The New Yorker* (10-12-2015).

Trento, Angelo and Silber, Irwin. *Press Box Red: The Story of Press Box Red: The Communist Who Helped Break the Color Line in Sports.* Philadelphia: Temple University Press, 2003.

Walker, Hunter. "Bernie Sanders on What He Learned from Brooklyn, Baseball and His Family's Immigrant Roots," *Yahoo News* (9-09-2019).

Wechsler, James. "The Coughlin Terror," *The Nation* (7-22-39).

Wilder, Craig Steven. *A Covenant with Color: Race and Social Power in Brooklyn*. New York: Columbia University Press, 2001.

Williams, Mason B. *City of Ambition: FDR, La Guardia, and the Making of Modern New York*. New York: Norton, 2013.

Williams, Raymond. "The Realism of Arthur Miller," in Robert W. Corrigan, ed. *Arthur Miller: A Collection of Critical Essays*. Englewood, NJ: Prentice Hall, 1969.

Wilstein, Matt. "Hillary Clinton Redoubles Bernie Sanders Attack on 'Ellen': Need Someone 'Who Can Win,'" *The Daily Beast* (2-6-2020).

Zinn, Howard. *The Politics of History*. Boston: Beacon Press, 1970.

ACKNOWLEDGMENTS

I extend my gratitude first and foremost to Larry Sanders. This book simply would not have possible without the many insights he patiently provided regarding his and Bernie's childhood in Brooklyn. Equally generous were Bernie's high school friends Myron Kalin, Steve Slavin, and Lou Howort, each of whom helped fill in details about both Bernie's life and their neighborhood. Like Bernie, all four of his contemporaries share an inspiring enthusiasm for life.

This project also benefitted greatly from the handiwork of my ace research assistant Urwah Ahmad. A recent graduate of St. Joseph's College in Brooklyn (who double-majored in journalism and political science), Urwah dug up more than a few useful nuggets from the era's newspapers. Brian Berger, who is writing a history of Brooklyn, generously relayed many insights from his work. I'm also grateful to Michelle Montalbano, reference librarian for the Brooklyn Collection at the Brooklyn Public Library, and Shannon O'Neill of the Tamiment Library for their most useful advice.

A wide range of scholars and archivists also furnished considerable assistance. For sharing their expertise regarding Arthur Miller, I'm indebted to Christopher Bigsby and Steve Marino. Will Kaufmann was happy to do the same concerning Woody Guthrie. Woody's granddaughter Anna Canoni of Guthrie Publications (woodyguthrie.org) and Kate Blalack of the Guthrie Center in Tulsa (woodyguthriecenter.org) were both extremely helpful. Meanwhile, Maurice Isserman, Gerald Meyer, Richard Greenwald, and Harry Clark helped clarify some of my points about the era's politics.

I would not have been able to complete this project without my sabbatical at St. Joseph's College in the fall of 2020. I'd particularly like to thank my colleagues Michael Hanophy, Raymond D'Angelo, Gail Moran, and Jeremy Cash (who, like Bernie and company, graduated from James Madison High School). At O/R, Colin Robinson and Emma Ingrisani made the book come to life. Special thanks to my pals Christian Parenti, Williams Cole, Doug Cordell, Alan Reeder, Diego Baraona, and Donald Breckenridge. And to my wife, Toni Cela Hamm, and our son, Ellis, for their steadfast love and support.

—T. Hamm
Sunset Park, Brooklyn
March 2020